AKASHA

Spiritual Experiences of Accessing the Infinite Intelligence of Our Souls

Enjoy these other books in the Common Sentience series:

ANCESTORS: *Divine Remembrances of Lineage, Relations and Sacred Sites*

ANGELS: *Personal Encounters with Divine Beings of Light*

ANIMALS: *Personal Tales of Encounters with Spirit Animals*

ASCENSION: *Divine Stories of Awakening the Whole and Holy Being Within*

GODTALK: *Experiences of Humanity's Connections with a Higher Power*

GUIDES: *Mystical Connections to Soul Guides and Divine Teachers*

MEDITATION: *Intimate Experiences with the Divine through Contemplative Practices*

NATURE: *Divine Experiences with Trees, Plants, Stones and Landscapes*

SHAMANISM: *Personal Quests of Communion with Nature and Creation*

SIGNS: *Sacred Encounters with Pathways, Turning Points, and Divine Guideposts*

SOUNDS: *Profound Experiences with Chanting, Toning, Music and Healing Frequencies*

WITCH: *Divine Alignments with the Primordial Energies of Magick and Cycles of Nature*

Learn more at sacredstories.com.

AKASHA

Spiritual Experiences of Accessing the Infinite Intelligence of Our Souls

LISA BARNETT

Copyright © 2023 All rights reserved.

This book or part thereof may not be reproduced in any form, stored in a retrieval system, or transmitted in any form by any means-electronic, mechanical, photocopy, recording, or otherwise without prior written permission of the publisher, except as provided by United States of America copyright law.

The information provided in this book is designed to provide helpful information on the subjects discussed. This book is not meant to be used, nor should it be used, to diagnose or treat any medical condition. The author and publisher are not responsible for any specific health needs that may require medical supervision and are not liable for any damages or negative consequences from any treatment, action, application, or preparation, to any person reading or following the information in this book.

References are provided for information purposes only and do not constitute endorsement of any individuals, websites, or other sources. In the event you use any of the information in this book for yourself, the author and the publisher assume no responsibility for your actions.

Books may be purchased through booksellers or by contacting Sacred Stories Publishing.

Akasha:
Spiritual Experiences of Accessing the Infinite Intelligence of Our Souls

Lisa Barnett

Print ISBN: 978-1-958921-29-6
EBook ISBN: 978-1-958921-30-2

Library of Congress Control Number: 2023940326

Published by Sacred Stories Publishing, Fort Lauderdale, FL USA

CONTENTS

PART ONE: UNDERSTANDING THE AKASHA

You Are an Infinite Soul 5
What Is the Akasha? 9
Your Soul Has a Library 15
Your Library Has Librarians 21
Wisdom from the Akasha 25
Learning on a Soul Level 49
The Quantum Field and the Akasha 59

PART TWO: SPIRITUAL EXPERIENCES OF ACCESSING THE INFINITE INTELLIGENCE OF OUR SOULS

My Life as a Whale *Lisa Barnett* 75
Ancestral Healing *Michelle McClennen* 79
Painting the Akasha *Sheryl A. Stradling* 87
Standing Out *Rebeka Lopez* 91
My Road to Freedom *Siobhan Maguire* 95
Pius Martin *Pamela Nance* 101
The Akashic Stone *Dr. Kurt Johnson* 107
Sea of Life *Linda Berger* 113
Waking from the Tidal Wave *Sandy Rakowitz* 117
Messages of Love *Erika Osmann Mason* 121
A Change in My Life *Stephany Levine* 127
Souls Interwined *Marcia Lowry* 133
Healer on a Healing Path *Caroline Lambert* 141
I Found My Mayan Temple *Devara ThunderBeat* 143

Healing Harmful Tapes *Renee Teresa* 147
Released from Ropes *Jenny Mannion* 151
Tuning In to the Akasha *Sophia Moon* 155
Just a Saturday Workshop *Jennifer Perez Solar* 159
A Seraphim Angel *Lisa Barnett* 163

PART THREE: DEEPENING YOUR EXPERIENCE OF THE AKASHA

Guided, Guarded, and Protected 171
Embodying the Akasha 189
Start Accessing Your Records 199
Our Galactic Origins 215
Awakening to the New Earth 221

MEET THE SACRED STORYTELLERS 227
MEET THE AUTHOR 231

PART ONE

Understanding the Akasha

The key to growth is the introduction of higher dimensions of consciousness into our awareness.

—LAO TZU

YOU ARE AN INFINITE SOUL

I invite you to join me as I introduce you to one of my great loves… the magnificent Source energy field, the Akasha. Ever since the first time I walked up to its gates, I have felt enamored with the mysteries of what it really is and how we are all part of it. For a long time, I wondered how I could get past its guards and reach the other side of the beautiful, gilded gates. With much persistence and intuitive guidance, I found a way to go beyond the gates and enter the Akasha. Ever since, it's been the ride of my life to discover, learn, heal, and grow.

And now it is your turn.

I first stumbled into the Akasha as an intuitive energy healer in the 1990s. I had studied psychic energy healing with a knowledgeable and trusted instructor for more than six years. As I performed a healing for someone, she would tell me to go up to the gates of the person's Akashic Record—to ask their record keeper for Akashic energy to fill them up after the clearing they had received from me.

But my teacher would admonish, "You can only go to the gates. You are not allowed inside."

Part One

When I stood there at the gate, asking the Akashic Beings of Light to fill my client up, I witnessed new energy flowing into my client's crown chakra and filling their body. It was a magnificent, sparkling, fluid light. I knew the energy entering them held higher wisdom, even though I wasn't sure what that wisdom was.

One day, I heard a deep voice telling me about my client's soul path and how their past lives were impacting the present circumstances and creating their challenges. The first time it happened, it wowed me! These beings showed me the great expanse of the client's life as their soul plan unfolded. I saw a 2,000-year timeline of who they had been and why they wished to be here on Earth at this time.

This was a different level of information than I had ever accessed as an intuitive healer. But where did this wisdom come from? In the '90s, no one was talking about the Akasha or accessing the Akashic Records.

On rare occasions, expansive information would come through while I was working with clients, but I couldn't predict when it would happen. It never occurred to me that it came from the Akasha, because my teacher had said the records were off-limits to us. I had no knowledge of how to get there on my own.

Years later, after a few spontaneous connections and many hit-or-miss attempts to consciously access the records, I finally found a simple way to open the gates and move into the Akasha. The impact of access to these profound records changed the trajectory of my life. It put me on a clear path of transformation that continues to guide me to this day.

Now, some thirty years later, I'm well acquainted with the magnificent wisdom and healing energy of the Akasha. Access to this wisdom unlocked my purpose, which is to share and teach others how to bask in its unconditional love while healing their most wounded parts.

My wish for you is to embrace this soul work with an open heart. As you discover its path, you will tap into your own connection to Source energy through the Akasha.

I promise to share stories, knowledge, experiences, and tools I have gleaned from the many years I've worked in the Akashic Records. This book is part of my soul's mission to help you discover a more intimate relationship with your soul and the Divine energy of the Akasha. We will build a relationship with your very own Akashic Record Keepers.

I want you to experience what unconditional love feels like. Let it embrace you as you learn, at a soul level, why you are here.

LET'S DIVE INTO THE AKASHA... HEART FIRST

I look forward to you joining me on this journey into the Akasha. There is much to learn as you discover and experience wisdom from the source you originated from, so many lifetimes ago. All you must do is come with an open heart and a sense of childlike wonder as you read, learn, and experience yourself differently.

You will also learn from the personal stories, written with love, by many authors who share their own experiences of the Akasha. Each story will give you a genuine understanding of what it was like for them to be vulnerable enough, if only for a moment, to let in the magnificent healing energy and wisdom that changed their lives.

Now let's quench your curiosity by exploring what the Akashic Records truly are.

WHAT IS THE AKASHA?

Imagine a place where humanity and beyond have access to vast amounts of information that have been recorded and stored—a place so massive that our human brain can hardly comprehend that it exists.

The Akasha is the manifestation of Source, just as you are a manifestation of Source. This energetic field of "the All" cannot be separated from itself. We are all part of the unity of the universe. We are not separated in spirit, but only by our experiences. This place is home to the unmanifested energy life uses to create itself.

Akasha is a Sanskrit word meaning *sky* or *ether*. It describes the field where all that has happened, is happening, and will happen is energetically encoded. It's a unified field that is within the field of all. As they follow their soul's unique blueprint, each soul will find that the energy of the unmanifested potential is ready, willing, and waiting to become manifest.

The Akashic Records, as part of the All, are connected to everything ever created. Its libraries are the information arm of Source. The volume of knowledge here is immeasurable in an indefinable way, because the records hold the energetic vibrational recordings of every life form ever to individuate. Humans are not the only ones with souls imprinted inside the

Part One

Akashic Records. All living things have a higher purpose for living, including animals, and so do sacred sites and even organizations.

When your soul embarked on its journey of individuality, it did not sever your connection to the All. You remain an integral part of Source. Information about every soul is stored within the Akasha, and its infinite knowledge is available to us.

That means that everything is automatically recorded for each soul—every word, deed, and thought they have experienced since their soul individuated from Source. Think of it as your history, your story recorded in the etheric field. Your Akashic Records hold information from your past lives as well. You can use this knowledge to understand your soul plan for this lifetime.

Whatever you, as an infinite soul, decide to learn, release, enhance, relinquish, amplify, uncover, and encounter, is your choice. How you utilize your time on Earth lies within your authority, because you possess free will. You can change the trajectory of your life plan at any time by making different choices.

THE AKASHA HAS BEEN KNOWN FOR CENTURIES

Many religious texts refer to the Akashic Records, although they use different names. For example, the King James Bible says in Revelation 3:5, *He that overcometh, the same shall be clothed in white raiment; and I will not blot out his name out of the book of life, but I will confess his name before my Father, and before his angels.*

Professor and scientist Dr. Ervin Laszlo, who is also the author of *Science and the Akashic Field* and *The Akasha Paradigm: Revolution in Science, Evolution in Consciousness*, writes: "A concept advanced by the Hindu seers thousands of years ago is an amazingly accurate anticipation of this development. The cosmos has a hidden dimension: the rishis called it the

Akasha. They said that the Akasha encompasses all the other elements: *vata* (air), *agni* (fire), *ap* (water), and *prithvi* (earth). It holds all the elements within itself, but it is also outside of them because it is beyond space and time."

In his famous treatise *Raja Yoga*, Swami Vivekananda wrote that the Akasha "is the omnipresent, all-penetrating existence. Everything that has form, everything that is the result of combination, evolved out of this Akasha … it is the Akasha that becomes the human body, the animal body, the plants, every form that we see, everything that can be sensed, everything that exists."

WHY HAVEN'T I HEARD MUCH ABOUT THE AKASHA?

There was a time on Earth, thousands of years ago, when there was great access to the Akashic Records. But during the Dark Ages, many misused and abused the information for personal gain, which was detrimental to humanity. The Akashic Record Keepers decided to limit human access to this knowledge.

People have used information from the Akasha to win wars and steal treasures from others. Because this violated the integrity of the Akasha, the record keepers who guarded over the records moved the vibration of the Akasha away from Earth. Only advanced spiritual leaders—wise men and women, monks, shamans, leaders of temples, and mystics—had access for many centuries, and only after decades of training.

Even though I was conscious that there was such a thing as the Akashic Record, I was shocked when I first realized the record keepers were speaking to me. Remember, my original psychic teacher told me they were off limits, and we could only go to the Akashic gate to ask the record keepers for Divine energy to fill us up.

One of the first questions I asked the record keepers was, Why are the records open now? Their answers were enlightening. They explained that it was now time to bring back the expansive wisdom and transformational healing energy of the Akasha.

THE DAWNING OF A NEW AGE

The record keepers told me the new alignment of the planets, sometimes referred to as the Age of Aquarius, was part of the reason. This alignment is making it possible for humanity to awaken and start transforming our world. The Akashic Record Keepers believe that as we move into the astrological sign of Aquarius, Earth will experience a new age where human consciousness will evolve into a higher understanding of truth and reality.

Astrologer William Lilly first coined the term "Age of Aquarius" in 1730; it has been popularized through pop culture references such as the song by the same name in the theatrical musical *Hair*. According to astrology, the sun moves into a new constellation every 2,160 years. That move starts a new age. We are moving out of the Age of Pisces and into the Age of Aquarius. In astrology, the sign of Aquarius is associated with humanitarian efforts, genius intellects, being individualistic, and being ahead of its time.

People born under the sign of Aquarius are original thinkers who strive for independence. They can also be rebellious, demand complete freedom from constraints, and have a desire to reform society. Aquarians can also have an affinity for technology, science, and pioneer discoveries. With this new energy alignment, it is believed that humankind will come up with brand new ideas and create inventions to assist in healing the planet. We will create abundant food and water for all, and clean up the pollution and other ecological travesties that humans have perpetuated on this planet for hundreds of years. We will recreate our world into a beautiful, healthy, thriving planet as we move into this new Golden Age.

The coming of the Age of Aquarius will bring an end to current intolerance and old collective beliefs that support creating strife and war instead of love and respect. Doing so will allow human consciousness to rise toward a new way of thinking that fosters more understanding and acceptance of one another.

The coming of a new age is a time for excitement as we celebrate the evolution of our consciousness. However, it's also essential to continue to grow by accessing new knowledge, learning from ancient wisdom, and developing new ways to transform old beliefs. That is why I'm so excited about sharing the gifts of the Akasha with you. Learning to access your own Akashic Record can help you grow in a direct and impactful way.

TIME TO ANCHOR HIGH VIBRATIONAL ENERGY

After giving me an in-depth view of the Akashic Records' history on Earth, the record keepers asked that I help anchor the energy back on Earth. They suggested I start an Akashic Record School to instruct students worldwide to access their personal Akasha. They explained that when thousands of people begin accessing this high-vibration energy and wisdom, it will speed up the anchoring and expand its access for more of humanity.

Imagine that the energy of the Akasha is like a hot air balloon floating far above the Earth. When countless people put their energy into connecting to or grabbing hold of the ropes attached to the balloon, they can pull the energy balloon much closer and eventually ground the balloon. It then becomes anchored to Earth, which allows others to safely get in and out of the balloon. That's what we're doing with the Akashic Records. The more people access their Akasha, the easier it is for others to do the same.

Over twenty years ago, when I started speaking about the Akasha, few people understood that term. In the past decade, I've seen the Akashic Records become more common in the spiritual world and more accessible to humanity. As time passes, it will be possible to access their Akashic Records with greater ease. I will share the effects resulting from a process my Akashic

Part One

Record Keepers gave me, for those who are ready to find their calling and greater love for themselves at a deep soul level.

WITH KNOWLEDGE COMES POWER

As you will learn throughout this book, the Akashic Records come with guidance on how to navigate its immense library of knowledge. The record keepers assist us through the volumes and volumes of our information as well as the vast amount of information in its many rooms of specialized knowledge.

Now that we have started to understand the idea of what the Akasha is, let's explore.

YOUR SOUL HAS A LIBRARY

*J*ust imagine, for a moment, an endless library filled with volumes written about our own histories. Pages and pages of who we were in our past lives, who we were connected to through our soul families, what we did, how we lived, where we lived our different lives, and what we accomplished or did not accomplish—including being the scribe to note all our deeds and actions, to both fulfill karmic contracts and also to create them.

But the Akashic Records are more than just books about our lives on Earth. We are all galactic travelers and have galactic libraries. We've lived in many dimensions and on many planets. We are all star seeds, hailing from all over these universes. The Akasha is home to all these libraries.

You have a personal, magnificent library of mysteries waiting for your discovery. Your records contain information and wisdom about your hundreds of lives on Earth and your thousands of lives elsewhere. It is there to help you achieve your life's plan and purposes. It can help you heal, so you can fulfill your destiny. And all you must do is find your way into it.

Part One

EXPAND YOUR VIEW OF LIFE

When I made my own journey into my Akashic Records, I knew that we, as a species, no longer needed to live on the wild roller coaster of chaos and trauma we now call "life." Instead, we have the capacity to experience life from a broader viewpoint, seeing all angles in the who, what, where, when, and how your choices are rooted. In your records, you can sense the self-love your soul had for you when it decided to incarnate at such a monumental time in history. It needs you, its vessel, to walk through these life experiences.

What could you accomplish if you knew there were beings who unconditionally loved and revered you for the path you walk as a human? Would you feel more confident identifying your true purpose if you knew guidance was available whenever needed? Can you trust that you are here for a purpose that only you can fulfill—because you are that important to the composition of the universe?

Read these pages knowing that magic is awaiting you inside your Akashic Records, as it can help you find your soul's path, release old thought forms, and let go of repeating emotionally charged traumas. Through these records, we have direct access to past lives and karmic patterns that are the root of many of our problems. The healing opportunities to reconcile the body, mind, and spirit are endless when working in the Akashic Records. The journey is truly a heart-opening experience.

The book you are reading includes many tools to assist you in accessing some of these spiritual growth experiences. In Part Three, you will learn about the benefits of using the source energy of the Akasha, and I'll describe my Five-Step Wisdom Prayer System to help you start accessing your personal Akashic Records.

When you learn more about your soul's work in the Akashic Records, you can heal and upgrade your life on so many levels, in so many ways. The record keepers' assistance facilitates an immediate transformational process to help with healing on all levels of conscious living. They can go to the root of the problem to help us clear any obstructions that limit living a fully abundant life.

That is what the Akashic Records can and will do for you. All you must do is say, "Yes, I am ready to consciously ask for help, because clarity is what I seek!"

Once you agree, the record keepers will take you by the hand and become your guides to the areas of life that require healing. The more you release old patterns and beliefs, the clearer your soul's plan becomes. This book is your opportunity to discover and use an uncomplicated, straightforward tool that will always be at your fingertips. As you open your heart to the Akasha, you will experience more love and abundance flowing into your life.

The Akasha's library offers a clear path to resolve issues that life inevitably throws in our direction. Knowing how to access this magnificent energy field offers hope that your experiences aren't all there is. When you can see the bigger picture of your life, your soul's knowledge will make it easier to release childhood programming, ancestral genetics, and past-life trauma. You will recognize that you have been on a detour to a less-traveled road... the soul's path. The Akashic Records are ready and waiting for your conscious connection.

YOUR MOST EMPOWERING TOOL

Many believe we have everything we need to live valuable lives aligned with our soul paths. Yet even though I had psychic gifts and healing abilities, I realized I was missing one simple yet powerful tool. This is the gift of this work. The Akasha helps you to empower your existing gifts and awaken to the ones that are still unexplored or unrealized. The best part is, when you move into the vibration of the Akasha, your energy vibration rises to unconditional love to support manifesting your most aligned soul journey.

Part One

I've never felt alone, nor that I've had to do this on my own. I know that often, telling friends or family what I am feeling doesn't make sense to them. But my Akashic Record Keepers understand and respond with heartfelt assistance.

I wish I could tell you about all the places your Akashic Records journey will take you, but I can only give you a sense of what to expect, because it is your unique journey. You can learn how to access the Akashic Records to find the path that brings you joy. You can find information that helps you release what you need to, to heal you and clarify the way. I can promise you that you have never felt such pure love as you will receive when you step forward.

In your life, you can clear and release, receive and accept, tear down and build up anything that keeps you from being the magnificent soul you are and doing what you are meant to do on this planet.

YOUR SOUL'S BEGINNING

Let's start at the beginning, your soul's origin… and how you came to have a recording of your soul's journey in a library in the Akasha field that is full of your life stories over many millennia.

Imagine that we were created so we could experience infinite possibilities. No single energy form can experience it all. As the Divine continues to expand infinitely, it creates billions of souls as well as more planets and universes to fill the expanding space. The Creator is creating more manifestations from itself.

The Akasha is the information arm of this source energy. It is where everything has been recorded and stored. I like to imagine that as I sleep, the experiences of my day are uploading to the library. Of course, that view is a bit simplistic, as no one knows *how* our lives are recorded in the Akasha. I am just grateful they are.

THE BOOK OF LIFE

The Akashic Records, also known as the "book of life" in some religions, keep track of every soul's journey from the time it individuates from Source until its final return home, merging into the unified field. In the beginning of our soul journey, we are huge souls existing in various dimensions for hundreds of thousands of years, living in the bliss of the All.

Once we come to Earth, we become entrenched in the energy programs, karmic patterns, and contracts that bind us to this world. Each soul individuation keeps incarnating until it has completed all contracts, karma, and experiences needed to finally be able to return home.

That is why we have hundreds of past lives with relationships and karmic soul contracts, with life lessons to grow from and complete. The completions can look like many different scenarios or take the form of different types of relationships. It doesn't matter whether you are an "old soul" or a new one; the Akashic Records hold all your thoughts, feelings, actions, and deeds from each lifetime. In other words, it collects and records all your history to track everything you have done.

Imagine each of your books represents a different lifetime. Oh, the stories your library holds! Maybe you were a wife, husband, shopkeeper, butcher, mother, fashion designer, farmer, writer, artist, healer, doctor, or inventor. The possibilities are endless, as you've lived so many lifetimes. Most people can only dream of who they were, what they did, and how they lived. But working in your Akashic Records gives you direct access to some of those lifetimes. The most valuable information comes from past lives that directly affect the life you're living right now.

If you are more of a techie, think of your library as a file stored "in the cloud." And just as the cloud that's connected to your smart devices, your records are password protected. So are your Akashic Records. They are guarded by the record keepers who protect our information. When we access

Part One

our own records, we need to use a sacred key to unlock its knowledge. You will learn more about that in Part Three.

Now that you have a clearer picture of your Akashic Records, let's learn more about your record keepers, your Akashic librarians. In the next chapter, we will better understand who these beings are and how they can assist you in your spiritual journey and personal transformation.

YOUR LIBRARY HAS LIBRARIANS

*T*he idea that I had a massive library with no one to guide me was daunting. However, when I started accessing the Akashic Records, I realized I was not alone. Instead, specific beings of light supported me. I refer to these energetic guides as Akashic Record Keepers and sometimes Akashic Masters or Beings of Light. As I began to communicate with them, I asked their names.

Their response was, *We are the Akashic Record Keepers. You may call us that. We are pure Source energy and light. We have chosen to serve all the souls wishing to access Akashic wisdom. We have yet to take our own soul journey. We have never been human, angel, or other dimensional beings. We hold no judgment of your journey. We are in support of you. We are the Akashic Record Keepers.*

I was relieved that my library had energetic beings which supported and facilitated my work in the records. It was a relief to realize that, since they were pure Source energy and love, they had no judgment of me or my questions.

I was so excited about having my own massive library with librarians to answer all the questions I'd been asking throughout my life. I immediately had questions about my purpose and path, my health challenges, and the loss of my soul sisters. I wanted to know about my family, my soul family, and many other relationships. There was so much to learn!

Over time, I came to understand that asking questions is a powerful tool to assist us in opening our hearts for greater understanding and healing. I asked *hundreds* of questions during those first years of accessing the Akashic Records.

WHO ARE THE AKASHIC RECORD KEEPERS, AND WHO ARE THEY NOT?

Many clients have asked their angels or other guides to take them to the Akashic Records. Some have wondered if their grandmother, who has passed, is giving them information from the Akasha. In my case, I wanted clarity from the record keepers for myself and all my clients, so I asked them to explain who they are and how access works. This is what they said:

As we explain to you who we are not, we hope to help with any confusion as you will also learn who we are. We are not guardian angels, as they are from a soul realm where many humans choose to be of service by becoming angel helpers, living numerous lives within the angelic realm. Humans do not become archangels, as they are permanent and infinite soul choices; even so, it is possible to receive help and guidance from the angelic realm, which may be your soul's home base.

Yes, your soul has a home base. Many of you will find the planet or realm your soul calls home when you work with us in your records. All of you are star seeds who came from worlds far away. Your Akashic Records hold the information of your soul's home, which we know many lightworkers would find beneficial.

Understanding the Akasha

We are Akashic Record Masters, not ascended masters, as that is the path from humanity to ascension. Ascended masters' souls came to Earth numerous times to learn, experience, and ascend the human experience, thus having an awakening. They then chose to return to Earth to share and assist in awakening others. Buddha, Jesus, Mother Mary, and many others have walked the paths to awakening. Now they help your transformation as ascended masters.

We are not your loved ones who have crossed over, as most human souls are still deep in personal learning and growth. As souls pass into the other realms, they are wiser and often become aware of what they want to learn, but they still are not enlightened. Therefore, receiving information and guidance from them is much like seeking wisdom from a wise elder; it might be useful, but it might not.

We are not your healing guides or spirit guides, as they, too, are souls traveling a growth path and may have great gifts in healing, although they are much like you when you are not embodied. You also have incredible gifts and talents. Many of you have chosen to spend time being healing guides for humanity.

We, the Akashic Record Keepers, are pure original source vibration and are the keepers of the Akasha and the records within the realm. We are here to imbue the access prayers and healing prayers we give you with the vibrational healing energy of Creator/Source/God. We have never been human or traveled in your earthly realms. We have chosen to stay as individuated souls in the grand library of Source, to guide and assist all souls on their journey.

We are the keepers of your soul's library. Know it is our greatest pleasure and wish to serve you when you learn to access your soul's Akashic Record.

THE MORE QUESTIONS… THE DEEPER THE ANSWERS

It doesn't matter where you start your soul work; It is most important to start on the journey, even though you will encounter twists, turns, and roadblocks.

Part One

All experiences lead to more questions and more clarity. The answers are all there for you to access and receive guidance on how to reach the goals you made for yourself at this time in history. So, what do you want to know about your time here on Earth?

Our Akashic Record Keepers are always there for us. They understand our struggles. They know how difficult it is to be in this dimension. They revere us for being spiritual vessels of Source, trying every day to do our best with our understanding of life on Earth. They have only unconditional love and respect for us. They will always answer our questions, knowing we are only occasionally ready to receive the complete answer. Through their passion, we learn about forgiveness for ourselves as we struggle to understand our journey with clarity and love.

They want to help us. This is their gift to humanity. They feel that by understanding the uniqueness of our soul's path, we will identify and move through our karmic patterns and soul learning more directly, so we can embrace love and exude the love that every soul is here on Earth to experience.

As I've learned over the years, there is truly an art to formulating great questions to ask our record keepers, to go deeper into our soul's work. It's essential to thank them for their unwavering commitment and support toward our daily journey. In the next chapter, I will delve deeper into other details preserved in your Akashic Record.

WISDOM FROM THE AKASHA

You are here to grow and progress as the ancient soul you are. The record keepers often point out that life is not random, and we do not have only one life to live. As ancient and infinite souls with hundreds of lifetimes on Earth, we come each time to learn, grow, and share our wisdom and talents to fulfill our purposes. Yes, we have more than one purpose for being here. And we decided all of this before we were born.

My work with thousands of people over the years has shown me that most souls live more than five hundred lifetimes before completing their work here. Yet we continue to return to Earth to finish the learning and growth that eluded us in past lifetimes. Our soul contracts with different individuals show up in our encounters with people, places, and situations. There is a feeling of familiarity toward someone before we even get to know them. I'm sure you've heard people say, "I feel like I have known you forever."

We have experiences that feel like a déjà vu moment. Like we've been there and done that before, even though it isn't in our living memory. There is a reason for those déjà vu moments… they happen because we *have* been here before. We know that familiar soul from other lifetimes or have traveled and lived in that country that feels so comfortable. Have you ever tried something new that came so easily, it felt like you were "born knowing" how to do it? Because you have lived hundreds of lifetimes, it makes sense that you have lived in many places on the Earth. You've known thousands of people and honed many skills.

Remember that your Akashic Record Keepers are here to help you track the information in the Akasha that will support your life. When you access your Akashic Records, they will answer your questions about this lifetime and any past ones directly affecting areas where you feel stuck or lost. One of the greatest gifts from accessing the Akasha is finally receiving answers to questions that have plagued you for far too long.

I want to share vital information from the record keepers about how life works here on Earth and what you wrote in your plan. Each soul is unique, and it might not be easy to single out one question about your history. They want to share the way you form your relationships at a soul level and the importance of these life connections. Your relationships are here to help you succeed on the path your soul had planned for you before you were born.

YOU HAVE A COMPLEX PLAN

Each time we decide to reincarnate to Earth, our soul creates a plan we will uncover during our life. We make our plans as infinite souls desiring to do great things in our lifetimes. We identify which gifts, talents, challenges, and other souls we will encounter in the upcoming lifetime. In addition, we come with soul contracts and karmic patterns to learn from, including soul family members to support us in uncovering those patterns.

Our soul plan gives us guidance, which is extremely useful when we face challenges or must make decisions that impact the direction of our lives. However, with the recurring roadblocks impeding our ability to succeed, we must forge forward until we become aligned with our path. That's where soul contracts are beneficial; they give us other souls to help us. Many people find it easier to relax when they know that other souls are here to support them on their journey.

You wrote contracts with people to be significant love partners, business partners, best friends, parents, children, or siblings. Some of these relationships come from your original soul family, and others don't. For example, our parents aren't always part of our soul family. We may not even have a soul contract with them in some lifetimes.

Your soul has so much knowledge and information for you to navigate in this lifetime. The reasoning behind your soul's choices becomes more apparent as you live its plan and let it guide you. Doing so offers you a deeper dive into finding answers to *why you are here*.

SOUL FAMILY RELATIONSHIPS

Let's go back to the idea that when we individuate from Source in the beginning, we have a group of souls that individuate with us. This is our soul family. These souls travel through the multiverses together. Here on Earth, they are often people in different relationships within our lives. A soul family member might be our parent, child, spouse, or best friend. Sometimes, our soul family members volunteer to be the challenging people in our lives. They are the people who trigger us to deepen our understanding and finish a karmic pattern that our soul wants to complete.

Most of us have decided to have relationships with at least a few soul family members. We write contracts with approximately thirty-five to fifty souls. Some are part of our soul family and others are unfinished contracts with souls from our past-life relationships. We sometimes arrange to support that person in this lifetime; sometimes, it's about learning from them or being their teacher. The options are endless for which roles they play in our lives. Other contracts have karma attached. That means there is a lesson to learn so we can grow, heal, learn to forgive, and often share what we've learned with others. That way, our soul can evolve from those challenging experiences.

CONTRACTS WITH PEOPLE TO SUPPORT EACH OTHER

We always write soul contracts—also called *support contracts*—to help other people. We come to assist other souls, and they return the favor by helping us. They might be our friends, business partners, or mothers-in-law. Life can be easier when we have a support contract with friends, coworkers, bosses, and other family members.

It's good to know that if you have a support contract with someone, it's because both of you desire soul support. You might be from the same soul family or have had many positive past lives together. There are also support contracts to be challenging to each other. For example, you might end up having a challenging support contract with an intimate partner that includes working through karmic patterns together. The big challenges in those types of relationships often center on karmic patterns involving trust, betrayal, love, anger, or fear.

Support contracts might or might not have karma attached. Contracts with karma attached are commitments to work through to the end, to reach love by letting go of negative emotions such as anger or hate. It's essential to know that souls work together out of love for each other, even though once we are born, we don't remember that we agreed to feel so challenged by them. Being a soul in a body is tricky but discovering the intricacies of relationship-building from a soul level is fun.

WE WRITE MANY CONTRACTS

The record keepers also say that most of us have twenty or more contracts to form significant partnerships. These might be with our family members, spouses, life partners, best friends, or business partners. We love to have soul family members around us, even though many of us don't recognize them as such. Some of our soul family members have taken on a challenging role with a karmic contract to act as our adversaries.

We make six to twelve contracts for intimate partnership, such as marriages, life partners, or lifelong friendships. We don't just have one "soulmate." The record keepers say if we only had one intimate relationship contract, on a planet like Earth with 7 billion people, it's unlikely we would ever find our one. Instead, we hedge our bets and make a dozen such "soulmate" contracts, to ensure we accomplish our soul work each time.

The record keepers have explained to me that what people think of as a "soulmate" might be a soul family member. We have known them for all our existence, so they feel like part of us—and in a sense, they are.

Over the time of our infinite existence, our soul family grows from a small group of forty or fifty souls to thousands of souls. There are always soul family members happy to make contracts with us. You can write thirty or more soul contracts with soul family members and other people you have karma to work on and not run out of souls to support you.

Think of how simple life was thousands of years ago. Today, our modern lives are full of travel, technology, careers, and jobs that take us to different countries, meeting many different cultures, religions, and races. Our soul families grow as the world changes, and as our soul evolves to fit in with the changes. During each lifetime, we grow and learn from the previous incarnations.

There are many subtle aspects of what we write into our soul contracts. For example, you may have a soul contract with your mother, but not with your father. You might choose a specific family for the love you'll receive and another family member to challenge you.

CONTRACTS WITH CHILDREN

Many families now are blended families. Some stepparents feel as close to their partners' children as they do to their own. They might wonder if they have a soul contract with a specific child in their partner's family. Or if there isn't a contract, why is the child in their life constantly challenging them? The challenged stepparent might be in a support contract. Surprisingly, you might have a soul contract with a child you don't meet until they are a teenager. The contract supports the soul's spiritual growth and was optional when they were younger. Then you become not only the stepparent but their mentor in life. Contracts are as unique as you are.

SOUL CONTRACTS FOR ADOPTION

Many children who are put up for adoption have abandonment issues, feelings of unworthiness, and fear of being unlovable. They might wonder why their birth parents gave them away. As souls, we set up challenging situations so we may continue our soul growth. The more complex the challenge, the more we will grow.

I've seen many lightworkers plan an extremely challenging life with adoption, abuse, and health issues. Part of their plan is to complete all the outstanding karmic patterns in this lifetime. When they understand that this was their soul plan, they are able forgive everyone necessary. Then they can complete their personal healing and finally release all their karmic patterns for good. This is a powerful way to tidy up the loose ends after eight hundred lifetimes, but it's not an easy way.

Adoption can provide an excellent option when the biological avenue isn't viable. The record keepers say that sometimes a soul wants to be born to a specific person who can't or doesn't want to give birth to a child. They might write a contract to be born to their grandmother, aunt, or much-older sister, so they will stay in the same family but be raised by someone else.

Sometimes, a birth mother contracts to have a child for the greater good of the world or for another soul. They have a contract with the other adoptive adult instead of with the child.

Adoption may involve the birth mom's trauma or a family control issue. The mother might be too young to care for a child, or she became pregnant from a rape and she doesn't want to have the child, much less care for it. These situations are based on our soul's desire to learn about intense emotions, understand trauma, make difficult choices, and overcome levels of emotional pain such as abandonment. These extreme traumas, coupled with the emotional pain, take many lifetimes to work through.

Eventually, working through it would mean feeling compassion and forgiveness for all involved, including herself. For example, you've been put up for adoption and a loving family adopts you. This time, you're happy and grateful to have lived with a loving family instead of with your birth mother, who is struggling with addiction. You don't feel unworthy because you can see the bigger picture. You forgive your birth mother for being unable to make a good life for both of you, and you're grateful she had the courage to let you go. Instead of feeling abandoned, you go on to create a happy life for yourself; you might even decide to pass on the gift of a loving home by adopting a child.

THE SOUL CAN'T BE DESTROYED

Another situation that many people feel is controversial is abortion. This is how the record keepers see it: When a soul first comes to Earth, it may try on a body a few times before staying embodied. That might look like a soul entering a body that miscarries or is aborted. The record keepers say that the soul usually solidifies its contract with the physical body late in pregnancy, sometimes even after the baby is born. The soul can't be destroyed through death. In the case of a soul looking to embody at a specific time, it may choose a new vessel in another family and continue with a revised soul plan. The loss of our children is heartbreaking, but please know that their souls continue.

The soul makes a contract with the body to be the vehicle or vessel, and they come together to create an embodied soul. When the body ceases to function, the soul moves on. That is true whether the life ends because of old age, accident, illness, or even abortion. The record keepers say there is no difference, because the soul is infinite.

They also add that, contrary to many religious beliefs, suicide does not damn a soul to a dark place. Suicide happens because the personality, the human aspect, is in extreme pain and believes it has no feasible way to heal itself. It is an unfortunate place to be, but the soul is not punished for exiting the incarnation.

After such a choice, the soul continues in soul school between lifetimes. They will follow up with similar challenges in other lifetimes until they can work through that karmic pattern to find compassion, forgiveness, and healing for themselves.

KARMIC CONTRACTS

If you were born into a challenging family with emotional issues and addictive patterns, you might have made a contract to come in and be supportive to them. At least one of the family members may be a soul family member with whom you made a contract to help overcome an addictive pattern that they have struggled with repeatedly in other lifetimes.

On this dense, human plane, we often struggle with our emotions and sensitivity. We may use alcohol or drugs as an escape. As a soul who has learned that karmic lesson, you might volunteer to be on the support team in the family, to help them understand their issue and get help. Or they may feel enough love to change their behavior and enjoy the love in the family instead of trying to escape through addiction.

You also may have come in to learn from them, and then to take what you've learned out into the world to help others through counseling, teaching, speaking, etc. It's interesting the infinite ways we write soul contracts with other souls. One of the things the record keepers want us to know is that even those we deem "terrible" people are still Divine souls struggling to find self-love and forgiveness.

PAINFUL LIVES

Remember, we are born with amnesia, so even though we wrote a plan, we stumble through life wondering why we have the worst luck in making money, finding love, or being healthy; when in our higher-dimensional lives, we are creator beings. Our experiences are more effortless in those worlds because we're embodying our infinite and powerful souls.

We write our intensive soul plans, then come and forget them. Part of the game on Earth is remembering that we are infinite souls and that this is a choice we made to experience this 3-D life. Many of us suffer because emotions can be so painful on this plane. We might feel abandoned by other people or even by Source. We feel alone in our pain.

Most people don't have a deep, Divine connection and can't converse with their higher selves, angels, or Akashic Record Keepers. They feel like they're in a body, alone and without guidance, just struggling to figure it out. This is why the record keepers and I want you to know that your soul did write a plan, and you are not a victim. We must see life, even our challenging experiences, as something we created to help us evolve.

For example, your soul plans a long life that includes creating clear boundaries and healing addictive patterns. Your life starts with a difficult childhood, born into a family with a narcissistic mother and an alcoholic father. As a teenager, you have addiction problems due to the stress in your home life. You can't deal with all the stress, so you wash your victimhood down with alcohol and drugs.

Since you don't remember your soul's plan to live a long life with boundaries and overcoming addictions, the dependence pulls you in. It is impossible to overcome without loving support. Finally, the challenges overwhelm the human body and the mind. The soul and body decide it's time to leave Earth because life is just too hard, leading the liver and body to give out.

The soul planned to live long, overcome, and complete karmic patterns with boundaries and addictions. You still need to accomplish that plan. But, from the record keepers' and your soul's perspective, there is no judgment or failure. Since the soul is infinite, it will try again another time.

WE ARE NOT VICTIMS

As sad as it is when we hear of someone dying of alcoholism or suicide, it helps to look at their death from the view of the Akasha. In doing so, we can understand the bigger picture and what happened at a soul level. No matter what a soul chooses, it continues to learn something from each lifetime. It is our responsibility to give our compassion and love to the family, to help with their healing.

THE BIGGER PICTURE

We also realize how important the information and wisdom from our library is in helping us see the big picture and in making different choices. In the previous example, your life may have gone as planned if you had accessed your Akasha. You would have understood that you were an empath and needed to learn how to create boundaries in stressful environments.

With that information, you may have embraced the challenges rather than distract yourself with your addictions. You would have asked questions to learn how to overcome addiction patterns still active from other lifetimes and how to complete and transform all that energy in this lifetime. This important soul information would have empowered you to make different choices rather than taking a drink. Or if the problem had already started, you would have sought help earlier by going to a therapist or an Akashic consultant.

My example is one of the fundamental reasons I am sharing this book with you. I want you to have many examples and tools at your fingertips to live a long, healthy, joyful life. Our Akashic wisdom has been brought back to Earth to help people living with unconscious pain and trauma. At this time in history, we need help to heal and remember the greater truth, so we can see and know without a doubt. Then we can help to transform ourselves and our world.

STUCK IN THE SMALL PICTURE

I was working with a client the other day who was feeling jealous and upset that her older siblings were successful in business and making a lot of money while she was struggling financially. She felt like a poor child that no one would help. As a result, she was wallowing in victimhood. Even though all three siblings, herself included, inherited the same amount of money in their twenties, the others were better in business than she was. She could never bring herself to ask for their business guidance. She was afraid they would judge her if she asked for help.

Instead of investing in a business mentor, she spent money on clothes, new cars, and remodeling her house. She continued to live as she had when she was a wealthy child. In her later years, she realized she had gone through all her money, while her siblings had made more money with smart investments. She became so angry, she no longer talked to her siblings. She blamed them and felt that they had done her wrong, even though she had never asked for their help or support. She held on to her anger by cutting them out of her life, which left her feeling lonely and sad. She waited for her brother and sister to either give her money or write her into their wills, even though she refused to talk to them.

If she could have seen the bigger picture and her soul's plan, she would have realized that what her soul wanted to learn was unconditional love. Her soul created this challenge so she could learn about karmic lessons and support contracts, including those within her soul family relationships. Her life was full of blocked energy that she could have released and transformed into empowering experiences.

Her soul was interested in learning about being vulnerable with others, giving and receiving emotional support, and even learning about the many aspects of generosity. All this would have uplifted her to a higher vibration of love for herself. She knew how to be generous with herself, but never with others. It was easier to be angry at them than at herself for not investing the money to ensure she would be financially stable in her later years.

I opened her Akashic Record and asked her record keepers to clarify this issue on many levels. We worked on clearing some of the emotional pain and trauma from her energy field and body. We even went back into her Akashic Record from childhood, where she held old beliefs that she wasn't good enough and that her mother didn't love her as much as she loved her siblings. As we cleared some of these aspects, she began to feel better about herself and her life. The record keepers asked, *Are you ready to forgive your siblings, to reach out an olive branch and create a loving relationship with them again?*

She answered, "No." She still felt hurt and angry, wanting to hang on to the pain.

One of our biggest human challenges is the vindication we feel when we wallow in low vibrational emotions such as pain, jealousy, guilt, and blame.

We want to tell everyone our sad tale in hopes people will understand and love us more. If we can see through the drama and our painful memories for what they are—distractions that keep us stuck in the yuck—we can then start making new choices and move forward on a path of change.

Each painful memory holds within it an opportunity to shift out of what we don't want and into what we do want in life. We can move from low vibrational energy, which makes it hard to see the bigger picture of our life, to the higher vibrational energy of forgiveness and love. The higher frequencies carry all our good. Letting go of the drama makes room for real love, so we can flourish.

The record keepers have asked me to bring the Akashic Record wisdom back to humanity to help everyone see that this knowledge is part of Earth's big awakening. Your soul holds the keys for human evolution. The record keepers want you to realize that the time is here for souls to gather and evolve together. We can do that by releasing traumas and emotional triggers like jealousy, blame, shame, and guilt. We are letting go of low vibrational emotions now and moving into a higher vibration of love.

No one forced us to come to Earth. We were excited to come and be part of a grand experiment. Our goal is to experience a life filled with the upgraded emotions of love, supportive relationships, and wonder. Receiving deeper knowledge through your Akasha will give you the freedom you have been seeking to support you on your journey.

If my client could have realized that she had been the one to mistreat her siblings by giving them the "cold shoulder," she might have realized that she played a part in her story and that it wasn't done to her. She orchestrated her pain.

When we realize it is our human ego that is saying no to forgiveness, we can shift into our hearts, where it is easier to find compassion and forgiveness. Just think of how much we could accomplish if we embraced more forgiveness. We would unlock so much stuck energy to use in manifesting new choices.

We can have so much fun playing in the game of life with our fellow souls—especially when we are unencumbered by low vibrational emotions.

FORGIVENESS IS THE PATH TO AWAKENING

It's time for us to understand that each of us is a Divine soul, no matter how we act in the world. When we really embrace this truth, we can create miracles in our own lives. No one says we must do this overnight. There are small steps we can take. When we start to see the bigger picture, it's easier to find the next baby step. Those cumulative baby steps are taking you to more happiness and connectedness through forgiveness.

One of the tools you will find later in the book is the Forgiveness Prayer. Reciting this prayer daily can do some of the heavy lifting. It will help you to let go of a jealous or angry heart. Even if you don't know what or whom to forgive, the magic will still happen. This one prayer will assist in letting go of judgment and hurt so you can begin to see everyone as a Divine soul. It's all about baby steps.

THESE IDEAS CAN TRANSFORM YOUR LIFE

First, you must be willing to let go of the old story. It's time to forgive yourself and others. You wouldn't be reading this book if you weren't interested in shifting into a higher vibration so you can find love and compassion with those beautiful souls you wanted to be in your life. Just start by loving yourself because that makes loving others easier.

No matter how horrible our life may look, there is always a small step we can take that will start the movement of change. The more we can lead from our hearts and let go of the belief that we are victims, the easier it is to find a different way to think or feel about making a new choice. We start to understand that we came here for a reason, and we want to support each other. We become empowered by supporting other souls. We may be their student in life's school or their teacher—and often, we are both.

Soul growth and learning can take place in every scenario. The critical piece is to complete the learning pattern of that challenge, which may have followed us through many lifetimes.

SERVICE CONTRACTS

We also write service contracts to be of service to the greater good. Not everyone chooses significant partners or children. Many souls come to be in service to a community or place. We may feel it is best to direct our service to our oceans or to the planet.

Sometimes, our calling is to support people who are not as fortunate as we are. For example, we might take someone under our wing and teach them some of what we've learned. We might help them financially or with physical services like driving them to the doctor or helping them move. Some of us were meant to be in service in our greater community or the country. We may decide to work at an animal care facility, help homebound people, teach adults to read and write, or aid at a homeless shelter.

Many of us are in service with our friends and family. When my children were teenagers, they often brought home friends who had problems with their parents and lived in ongoing stressful situations. There were times they needed a night away where someone could see and hear them differently. I knew that part of my life's work was to serve these young people by holding a space of unconditional acceptance for them as they grew up, helping them feel loved by people in the world, even when their parents couldn't give them the love they needed. It was an honor to be in service to these souls.

People may wonder if there really is a reason for having endured so much emotional pain. The record keepers tell us that every experience has a purpose. Those traumas and challenges will lead to something more significant in life, if we are open to the lessons bearing gifts that can appear on the other side of that pain. We can overcome feelings of unworthiness by sharing our stories and wisdom to serve humanity. When one goes through a lifelong trauma like childhood abuse, they might want to share the knowledge they've gained. You might even inspire someone to speak up and end their abuse.

So many souls have overcome abusive childhoods and gone on to uplift others in their careers and jobs. They've learned how vital their story of challenge and healing has been. Some people have become therapists or healers, while others work with friends and family to support them by helping heal their pain and trauma so they can share their own gifts.

PAST LIFE GIFTS

One of the joys in life is to discover the latent gifts we have. We've honed these gifts with expert precision over hundreds of lifetimes. Imagine what our ancient and infinite souls might have planned for us in this lifetime. Since we don't remember anything we have done or been in our past lives, we get to spend this life on the path to self-discovery. We try out different roles to find the ones that fit exactly right.

Like many of us, you may not believe we only get one chance to get life right. I was so grateful to learn that we have multiple opportunities to incarnate. Life in this dimension is full of so much to discover, learn, and create. Are you excited to find out how you can excel as the unique soul you are?

It's exciting to think that I may have been an inventor, a painter, a singer, an engineer, a writer, a scientist, a builder, or an architect in other lifetimes. We have all lived hundreds of lives; most have tried it all, succeeding at some endeavors and failing at others.

When we decide to come back again, part of our planning process is to identify the natural gifts, training, and skills that align with our mission to share on Earth. First, it's a process of researching our records to find some of the unique talents we have developed over many lifetimes. Then we can decide which of those we want to use in this life and which others we want to develop. We might take at least four to six talents with us into each lifetime.

We might discover a few of these talents early in life, in college, at work, or much later. Some experience this as an unveiling, while it is an obvious knowing for others. Take a moment now to think about things that come to you easily. You might have found you have a knack for painting, photography, chemistry, biology, writing, or even raising children. For example, do you find being a parent the most fun and joyful thing you could do? Parenting might have been something that you looked forward to when you were young.

Some women have soul contracts to be the "mother of all" instead of the mother of one or two. Those are often women who hold a higher vibration of the Divine Feminine, helping other women to step more fully into their power as feminine goddesses. Others may help spread the love in less fortunate countries, which need people to feed, raise, or adopt orphaned children. They might feel called to help less fortunate children feel loved, learn to read, have healthy meals, be well-clothed, and have other enriching life experiences.

Of course, there are always thousands of ways to write a soul contract. Remember, we have free will in choosing how we share our gifts. Each person who brings a group of skills and talents will use them differently than someone else with similar gifts and talents. The record keepers love to remind us how unique we are and that there is no truth to the idea of competition as the way to "win" the game of life. We have our own contracts to fulfill and support contracts to help us along the way.

Whatever you find great joy in may be part of your purpose if it aligns with your soul's work. In planning this lifetime, you wanted to share an accumulation of your gifts and talents with humanity or with your friends and family. You might take your skills out into the world through your business, non-profit, or volunteering. Your talents and gifts came with you for a reason. It's up to you to unlock the secret missions your soul has for you as you discover your magnificent self.

SEARCHING FOR YOUR SOUL'S PURPOSE

As we have noted, thinking about the things that come effortlessly to you can be constructive if you are searching for your soul's purpose. For example, someone who loves to cook and feed others may choose to become a chef, open their own restaurant, or work in the kitchen of a homeless facility. Another person who loves to write may author books or they might become an editor or a professor and teach others to share their gifts through writing.

Our purposes—yes, we have more than one—are never hidden from us; all we need to do is reflect on what brings us joy. Many people say they are looking for their life purpose. The truth is that everyone has many, which include working with your numerous soul contracts, using your gifts and talents, and being the high vibrational light that you indeed are.

I have felt blessed to do Akashic readings for people who wonder what their soul's purpose is now that they've retired from work. They may learn from their records that they have been walking their purposeful path all their life and it is now time to enjoy the fruits of their labors. They can relax as they share their love with the world, bringing their light wherever they go and to whatever they do.

Our purposes are not necessarily complex, although there may be some challenges along the path to clear the way for the soul to become fully present in the joy of living on purpose. I hope you will see your challenges as doorways, leading to a fulfilled, purposeful life, and find those challenges exciting to conquer.

THE FUTURE SOULS

The record keepers say that many children coming to Earth in the next fifty years will remember who they were and what gifts they developed from their past lives in other dimensions and worlds. Our world will need their specialized abilities to change the trajectory of the Earth. They will have direct access to the information needed to be the inventors that help heal our planet.

Many will have service contracts with our planet, finding ways for Earth and its inhabitants to survive together. For example, they may invent ways to take the saline out of the ocean water so that we can access more water worldwide. Some will help us with the pollution in the air or in the land. Some will find ways to transform plastics into something usable and sustainable. The record keepers say that there will be millions of children coming to help us as we go forward, creating a new Earth and into the future.

ANOTHER LOOK AT TRAUMA AND SOUL GROWTH

There is so much trauma and pain in our world. Wanting to understand it from the view of the soul's journey, I asked my record keepers to educate me on why so many people suffer in this dimension. They replied that trauma can lead to an understanding that we must not be a victim of it, but instead remove ourselves from the source of pain and heal the parts we feel are still painful. When we seek help and trust we will find support and love as we walk the path of healing, we remember we are not alone. Again, it's about baby steps.

The healing of trauma unlocks a potent energy for creating a new way to live. The record keepers also told me that pain and trauma can motivate us to do something radically different when we come to a point where we just

Part One

want it to stop. Powerful actions can happen when one is tired of being angry, scared, frustrated, and hurt. But often, we just don't know how to change or what new choice to make. The record keepers want to show us the way.

You can decide to make new choices when you have endured enough and you can't take it any longer. One option may be to crawl into bed and hide under the covers, hoping everything changes and life will look different when you get out of bed. Unfortunately, in that scenario, there isn't any action to clear the energetic patterns, so stuck you will stay. We continue to view ourselves as victims of a terrible world. People who can't look beyond the pain might stay stuck until it's time to leave the physical world.

A productive way to change would be to do something, anything positive that moves you in the direction of ending the cycle. That one powerful choice—saying "This will never happen again"—will change the trajectory of your life. This choice takes a huge investment of energy and ignites the soul contracts of those who promised to come forward to help facilitate the change. Remember, the different possible scenarios are endless because the options are based on what the soul wants to accomplish in the current lifetime.

Seeing people in pain or who have been through traumatic situations is heartbreaking. We want to get back at the perpetrator, to give punishment where it is due in our human sense of justice. But, when we look at those situations from the view of the soul, there are more dynamics in play. Each one is as unique as the souls involved, from the supportive roles to the perpetrator roles.

From the soul plan and soul's point of view, the soul who contracted to impart pain on another does so by giving up a life where they could have been a good and loving person. Instead, they chose to be the one who helps other souls stop the cycle of trauma and pain by perpetuating it to a level where change happens. When the traumatized soul says "no more," it releases all souls involved from the karma and contracts, so they are free to make new choices.

Karmic contracts, support contracts, and soul family contracts are in action to help each of us evolve. Remember, we made these commitments before we were born with the greatest love and highest intention to help each other release latent energy from the past to succeed in their life.

You might struggle for much of your life. However, please know that these challenges are not meant as punishment. Instead, we wrote these painful situations into our soul plan because we want to experience both sides of every imaginable scenario in our world. As an infinite soul, we don't see things as good or bad, and there is no right or wrong.

WHY WOULD MY SOUL CHOOSE TO INFLICT PAIN?

When I watch my twenty-five-year-old son play video games, I often wonder why such a happy and kind person finds it fun to play a video game with war, guns, blood, and destruction. Why would he enjoy playing a game with so much killing?

I've learned this is an excellent example of how we feel when we are infinite souls choosing to go on a journey to Earth again. We might be the loving person in some lifetimes and are curious about what it is like to be the villain in others. Sometimes we want to be the healer or the doctor, while other times, we decide to be the destroyer, the abuser, or the aggressor. We might try to destroy our world and the people in it—not because we are bad people or evil souls, but because it is the game we play as infinite souls. Looking at life from a broader perspective, we can understand that, as souls who have been on Earth more than five hundred times, we have done it all and want new experiences.

We have been the destroyer and have been the savior. Yet, we are genuinely creator beings, impacting every aspect of life we can. As you read this, let yourself take a breath and drop into your heart center, knowing you have lived as both a creator and a destroyer. It can be a painful realization if you've never thought of yourself as being someone who isn't kind and loving. But from the soul's viewpoint, there are no good or bad moves in this game. The outcome is always positive because it helps us grow.

One of the reasons we come to Earth is to raise our vibration to the highest level of love. Yet, so often, when a client comes to me wanting to know why they would pick this terrible life, the record keepers respond, *Because you wanted to have that experience to trigger you to do something different with your life this time.*

It is a gift to work in your records or receive a professional consultation that helps you see the bigger picture. You can shift to a higher frequency of love and forgiveness when you clear the stuck energy from emotional pain and trauma. Access to your Akashic Records opens you to the information behind the trauma, making it easier to let go of the pain. The pain can be a springboard to doing something great with what you've learned. Remember, when you clear old karmic patterns, you let go of the idea that pain is somehow a punishment. When you see it as a gift, you can transmute the old pain and use it for the greater good.

FOLLOWING THE SOUL'S LEAD

As humans, we often become impatient. We try to jump steps to get to the end. But really, what is the end? We all want to know what the next step will be. But everything in the universe must happen in order, including our soul work.

For example: Let's say your soul plan is to complete a karmic pattern from other lifetimes of infidelity. You plan to have a loving and supportive, long-term relationship with a spouse you had in a past life. During that past-life marriage, you had an extramarital affair. Now, to work through the karma—

extramarital affair, emotional pain inflicted on partner while married, lack of self-love—you will write a contract with the spouse from the past life with the intention of healing the past trauma and ending a complex karmic pattern.

In this life, you meet in college while getting your Ph.D. in Science, because you have a soul contract to become a science professor. You fall in love and decide to get married. Years later, as a science professor, you find yourself attracted to a student. The student has a contract with you to tempt you into an affair. You decide to have an affair, but before actually going through with it, you change your mind. That moment releases the karma pattern from past and present lives. You have made a new choice, to be faithful this time, and that has cleared the pattern with your spouse. The soul contract with the student is also complete.

Of course, I've simplified the portion of a soul's plan to explain how we align with our mission by following a sequence of steps. Each step leads to new choices that will set us on a new path with unknown blessings and experiences. Working in the Akasha to receive guidance about our contracts helps us to avoid an emotionally driven choice, such as the affair. We can then make new choices with greater insight into the questions of our life. Knowing about the karmic patterns eases our stress. Using the knowledge from the Akasha, helps us have the wisdom to find the right orderly path to end and release karmic patterns that have kept us unhappy and lonely in many lifetimes.

YOU ARE A PURPOSEFUL SOUL

Remember, you have many purposes. Every relationship also has a purpose, including your relationship to yourself, your career, your friends, and your family. All of these contracts are meant to help you fulfill your missions, whatever they may be. We each created a plan and asked other souls to join us to ensure we would succeed on our higher mission. Many stepped up to

Part One

commit to helping us, knowing we would also help them along the way. It's all personal to each soul. We knew we would have plenty of help and support.

I'd like to imagine a world where we all decide to be of service in helping heal the Earth and guide its inhabitants progress to a better way of life. I'd love to know that those souls of our future return to Earth knowing their unique soul plans and are prepared and driven to serve a higher purpose.

If we all choose to create Heaven on Earth, we will transform and awaken the planet in one lifetime. It can happen.

LEARNING ON A SOUL LEVEL

*E*very soul is Divine Source energy, manifested from the Akasha. We are an individuation of Source. We all wear body suits as we play the game of life we wanted to experience. After we leave this life, we will gather with the souls who have played their roles in our life, to thank them for their service. Imagine high fiving each other for all the lessons learned and goals reached. We come into each life with a variety of souls who have pledged to support us, just as we do for others. But what are their roles, and why do they do it?

People often ask me, "Why would I pick this challenging relationship or parent?"

Sometimes we come to learn about compassion and forgiveness in a lifetime, because we may have been unkind, even mean, and emotionally abusive to people in a past life. If that were your plan, you might choose people who are cold or abusive, and possibly narcissistic, to play roles in your game of life this time around. If one of the lessons you needed to learn was about forgiveness, you would put many challenging people in your life.

Our responsibility is to allow ourselves to learn and grow from a human state of emotions, such as fear, anger, hatred, and lack of a state of forgiveness

Part One

or lack of compassion. We set up some of our soul contracts to work through those human emotions and to heal some of our relationships with emotional, karmic patterns attached. I've seen many souls decide to finish all their leftover karmic patterns in one life. Let me tell you, that looks like chaos—with PTSD to top it off.

When we connect to our record keepers, they educate and heal us at the root of the emotional karma to make our path easier. They often will unlock the energy to free us from its enmeshment or offer us more information about why we chose that specific challenge and how to untangle ourselves. We get stuck in our emotional pain because of our small view of life. Our record keepers take us outside of the experience and into the larger picture from the Akasha, so we can see what is at play with the dynamics in our relationships and their highest potential. Only when untangled from the emotional ties can we see the true purpose of the trauma or challenge. At that point, we can make a new choice, releasing blocked energy, thus changing the old pattern to something more aligned with how we want to live.

A simplistic explanation for our trauma in life is this: We plan these challenges so that we can evolve as a soul. Learning comes from challenges. When we overcome obstacles, forgive, and share our wisdom, we complete our karmic soul contracts or patterns. The record keepers often say that if life were easy, it would feel boring.

As you face your challenges, remember that your soul is growing and gaining wisdom and you will likely share your wisdom with others during your lifetime.

KARMIC PATTERNS

I believe that karma is misunderstood. Karma is a way for us to grow. Consider it as a tool for learning and growing at a soul level. It is not a punishment or something to fear. Karma can take lifetimes to complete, although it can happen immediately, in some instances. For example, we must work through the karmic patterns around emotional trauma, abuse, or betrayal in layers, taking many lifetimes to heal, clear and transform.

When we experience challenges causing mental, emotional, or physical trauma as part of the growth our soul desires, our questions about why we picked this challenging life filled with survival issues and trauma becomes irrelevant. We get to work—and that's when we learn.

As I explained earlier, we can write our soul contracts to include karma, which means there is an old story that we are still stuck in. We can't grow out of victimhood when we stay stuck, believing it's someone else's fault. Like a karmic hamster's wheel, you keep going around and can't figure out if there is any way off. The more you spin, the more frustrated you get, because you haven't yet figured out it's a karmic pattern.

Karma creates energy blocks that stop us from moving forward. It's like a roadblock rather than a detour. Working in the Akashic Records removes roadblocks by identifying the pattern, who is involved, and its relevance to the here and now in your life. Karma works in many ways—but, contrary to what many people think, it is not a punishment for something they may have done. It does not cause "bad things" to happen unless those experiences are things you have chosen because they will help you grow.

HITTING A BRICK WALL

Sometimes, karmic patterns show up as powerful life lessons. Sometimes, we get little reminders that it's time to shift our way of being in the world. If we miss the soft nudge, it may grow into a more prominent call to action. For example, here's a scenario that proved to be a quick karmic lesson a friend had while driving her car. If she hadn't been aware that the universe speaks in many ways, she might have had a more damaging car accident, which would have been a much bigger karmic call to action.

Part One

Julie's lesson came from a literal brick wall. I'm sure you've used the analogy of "hitting a brick wall" as a symbol of encountering an obstacle that will not move. Luckily, when Julie hit a brick wall, it just hurt her bank account.

This happened during a time in Julie's life when she was over-giving to family members and under-giving to herself. After months in survival mode and exhaustion, she inadvertently stepped on the accelerator instead of the brake when pulling into her parking space. As a result, she crashed into the brick wall just a couple of feet in front of her. Julie said she felt like she was in a dream when it was happening, as if the car had a mind of its own.

Julie then spent months not understanding why she hit a wall with her car. When she had an Akashic consultation, she learned of an old karmic pattern of feelings of unworthiness that kept repeating itself. Her unconscious lack of self-worth pushed her to work long hours, to cook for her adult children and grandchildren, and to generally make sure everyone she knew was happy, so they would respect and love her. Driving into the wall made her realize how little awareness she had about her exhaustion: her need to keep everyone happy, to prove her worthiness.

This karmic pattern had engulfed all areas of her life in obvious and subtle ways. She'd had a few quick and clear-cut reminders earlier in the year about the pattern, but she hadn't been willing to look at them. Her survival mode was too strong around worthiness. It took literally "hitting a brick wall" to wake her up. By listening to her record keepers, she realized she could let go of overdoing and still feel loved. That gave her the energy to take care of herself first.

Karmic patterns keep showing up because the soul wants you to act in a new and different way. As challenges arise, remember, the soul seeks a good life filled with love and joy. Your soul also knows its plan is meant to overcome challenges, traumas, and issues that stand in the way of the life your heart desires. When we aren't aware that our misery is related to karmic patterns, we feel like victims. We forget that, as an infinite soul, we chose those experiences to remember our strengths and how courageous we are, to empower us to fulfill our mission.

As your understanding of karmic patterns and soul growth expands, you will know what karma is and isn't and where to find it in your relationships with money, work, and family. It's an adventure—but one so well worth it!

THINK OF SOUL WORK AS EARTH'S SCHOOL

As your soul evolves from different lifetimes, it can go to other worlds and dimensions, sharing Earth's experiences. Think of it as progressing in school. You start with preschool and then work your way up to a Ph.D. in life. After that, you choose how far you want to go. It's all determined by what your soul desires to create in each lifetime.

We come to Earth to learn about compassion, gratitude, and forgiveness so we will eventually live in a state of awakening or enlightenment with pure, Divine love. We find our soul families. Then we sometimes go through trauma in our relationships, to get to forgiveness and love. But most importantly, we learn to forgive ourselves for squeezing our magnificent, vast souls into tiny bodies that do not represent who we are as individualizations of Source.

The Akashic Record Keepers often remind us that we are here to be of service. This is another reason for the many experiences we have during our lives. Our experiences provide information and guidance as we embark on a conscious path for greater truth. The magnificent gift from our Akashic Records is the expansive view of information and healing that can release us from the emotional pain and chaos this dimension often causes.

The Akashic Records information helps us finish past life lessons relating to trauma so we can release stuck emotions. The Akasha helps us heal by realizing that unconditional love surrounds us. Then we can clear our karmic patterns that can show up in our lives in many ways, casting us as perpetrators or victims. We might be working on self-love and forgiveness as we feel victimized, but also shame for being a perpetrator. These roles might show up in our relationships at work, with our family members, or in our love lives. Once you open your Akashic Records, you can determine the links that connect the here and now to your unfinished past lives.

Our soul keeps returning until we've learned to be conscious of our acts, words, and deeds and have crossed over into a state of joy and love, leaving the world a better place than when we entered it. We will repeat our lessons until we stop harming ourselves and others by making a conscious choice to stop, learn, and love.

LOVE MAKES OUR JOURNEY EASIER

Our emotions are extraordinarily complex and held deep within us. If we go through lifetime after lifetime ignoring and suppressing our feelings, they will show up at some point, wreaking havoc in our relationships or in our health or mental outlook. Illnesses are often the consequence of long-term, suppressed emotions.

The cliché "Love makes the world go round" isn't only about the world we share, but also about our inner world. The fastest way to heal is through love. That is one of the reasons healing happens so spontaneously within the Akashic Record, because it is a space filled with unconditional love. There isn't any judgment—only assistance.

Plenty of research has shown that poorly managed negative emotions are detrimental to our health. For example, negative attitudes and feelings of helplessness and hopelessness can create chronic stress, which upsets the body's hormone balance and depletes the brain chemicals required for happiness. Mental stress also damages the immune system, which, over time, can lead to illness and physical pain.

Our inability to give or receive love or relate deeply with others is another effect of low vibrational emotions. When we identify our traumas and free that energy through awareness, healing, and forgiveness of ourselves, we can return to a natural state of love. Another benefit is that our creative energy starts to flow, activating our connection to the abundance of all we are to experience in this life.

The soul plan considers what suppressed emotions we need to energetically release. What we experience in relationships prods us toward learning to pay attention and overcome. When I access the Akashic Records, I often see that the client's biggest block to creating a happy and prosperous life stems from childhood or past-life traumas of which they are unaware.

Here is a powerful mantra you can recite for thirty days, to remember your soul's truth: that you are an individuation of Source. Take a moment to put your hand over your heart, close your eyes, and take a deep breath as you say to yourself: *"I am an infinite soul, having this human experience. I grow and awaken with ease and grace. All is in the perfect Divine right order."*

Repeat thrice or continually as a mantra, especially when feeling stressed. It may be beneficial to repeat often, to remember who you are as an infinite soul.

REFRAME LIFE CHALLENGES

When I was younger, my two best friends died. In one way, I felt abandoned by them; in another, I felt like a failure because I couldn't save them. In my worst moments, I felt unworthy of having been the one who lived. Why did I survive? And why did they die?

My ego told me I couldn't help them and that they had left me. After these traumas, I decided to throw in the towel on life. I slid into an unworthiness pattern that many have experienced during traumatic periods in their lives.

I was plagued with thoughts that if I couldn't save them, then I was unworthy to go on to fulfill my soul plan as a healer. I was angry at God for taking my teenaged soul sisters from me. I found myself blaming God as well as myself. But at that point, it never dawned on me that their deaths had nothing to do with me. I was grieving too much to understand what their souls might have planned. My heart was too broken to see beyond my pain.

We are often egocentric and believe that everything is about us. However, the years of talking to the Akashic Masters have taught me that each soul has its own plan, which includes support for others and learning from our many relationships. We still make choices based on our free will, but eventually, we return to our soul's plan to learn and develop more compassion and love.

As a traumatized, abandoned, and angry nineteen-year-old girl, I decided that my punishment was to give up my esoteric beliefs and be human, with all the feelings. No more searching for my galactic home and higher meaning for me! Instead, I chose to do whatever humans do. At that moment, I decided to place my heightened conscious awareness and all the gifts I had come to share into an imaginary shoebox. For years, I hid this awareness on an etheric shelf.

You may have done something similar. If you didn't tuck your gifts and memories of who you were into a shoebox, maybe you did something more dramatic. It is possible that, when you were little, you were conscious of the incredible cosmic expanse—but then life beat you down. Did you see and talk to angels or fairies? Did you communicate with family members who had crossed over? Did they visit you to offer love? But then, someone told you that was silly and you shut down your clairvoyant and clairaudient gifts.

Maybe you had unloving, distant, or cold parents—not because they didn't love you, but because they didn't know how to love. They might have been victims of their own unloving parents and they continued to be emotionally traumatized adults. To your child-self, feeling unloved can often lead to the false belief that you are unworthy of a good life. We label ourselves inadequate when we don't receive the love that we want and need. These are all false thoughts and beliefs. No negative evaluation of you is valid from the soul's perspective.

Your Akashic Record gives you a more comprehensive picture of what is going on, to help facilitate the answers you need to learn more quickly and release the emotional pain.

YOU HAVE THE SUPPORT OF THE UNIVERSE

Don't ever underestimate yourself and the power of your soul's wisdom. You are a complex and ancient soul looking to evolve. Give yourself the space to continually expand your experiences, to go outside of what you usually think you should be; instead, look more deeply into your challenges to discover the gifts held within them.

You have the ability and the support of the universe to clear karmic patterns, align with your highest soul plan, and fulfill your soul's desire to transform your life into a life of love, support, and joy.

THE QUANTUM FIELD AND THE AKASHA

When I started accessing the Akasha, the idea that we had lived hundreds of lives—not just five or ten—was mind-boggling. It took years of experience in the records before I started feeling I had a good picture of how our soul world works. One of the questions I asked the record keepers was to explain where they keep the Akashic Records. I also wanted to understand how and why we work as an infinite soul, and how we choose our various incarnations.

They explained we want to play in every realm. We live an array of lifestyles, including paupers, royalty, prophets, farmers, artists, alchemists, etc. Occasionally, in one lifetime, we go from goddess to enslaved person—or vice versa. All of us have been both genders: 60 percent male to 40 percent female or 70 percent female to 30 percent male is typical. It's rare to see a soul who is 90 percent of one sex to 10 percent the other. But, of course, there is every exception possible, as we love being unique!

My curiosity had me wondering if we just came to Earth or if there were other places we lived. This was an uncommon question thirty years ago, and I had no one else to ask but the Akashic Record Keepers. Because they are pure Source energy and love, they have no judgment and would always answer my questions with truth. They also have a great sense of humor. They will explain esoteric concepts through stories that illustrate how things work. This is one of the stories they told me.

BECOMING A SINGULAR SOUL

I asked them how a soul individuates as an aspect of Source to become a singular soul. Below is a simplified version of how our individuated life begins for all of us:

Imagine Source as a tall, energetic, high-rise building in New York City. At one point, an aspect of Source chooses to individuate from the one field of Source. This energy gathers with a group of souls who also decide to individuate simultaneously. All want to know what it feels like to become an individual, make choices, and understand what 'self' means without Source.

As the first step, all of you get into an elevator at the top of the high-rise. You are moving toward individuating, and this small group of new souls becomes your soul family. As you ride the elevator toward the ground floor, you share your hopes and dreams about becoming an individuated soul with a soul family. You enter the elevator as a group mind, but when you arrive at the lobby level, you are entirely individual.

A plan begins formulating the following steps as a soul family. Each of you is curious about all the experiences and possibilities in a multiverse filled with so much. Where shall we explore? What shall we do? How do we move forward? When will we meet again? What's next? So many questions, so much wonder, and curiosity. Since none of you has experience outside of Source, you decide to stroll down the avenue, taking in all the activity from your senses.

As you walk, you see a large structure, one block square and about five stories high. Curious, all of you go inside to discover what answers it offers. After entering, you can't help but notice the thousands of books on each terrace, floor after floor. All of you look up as you circle around, taking it all in. It's breathtaking. Curious about what those books may share, you all decide to stay, study, and get the answers you seek to your many questions.

From those books, you all learn what possibilities lie ahead for the next part of your journeys, together and separately. Some go their way quickly while others stay and help in the library. You continue learning and understanding the world.

The large building with thousands of books represents our Akashic Record library and is an example of what is available to all of us. Our soul's library is part of Source vibration and holds all the memories and recordings of everything. The thoughts, words, deeds, and energetic resonances of our experiences fill our books.

Each soul eventually decides to plan its next adventure. Most souls go off into the multiverse to experience life in many other forms. A few souls stay in the library to become the Akashic Record Keepers in service to other souls.

They tell me that I worked as a record keeper for a while before going on my journey. That is why I could hear them, and they could connect with me, before it was common knowledge.

HEALING THE PAST

People often come to me because they decide it's time to let go of their childhood trauma, which makes them feel stuck. They also know it's from other lifetimes, but they have no resources to release it.

Let's expand your knowledge on healing or changing your stuck emotional pain through this quantum field of energy. Take a moment to imagine when there was no space or time. You are a part of Source with no history or identity. And then your soul decides to individuate from Source, taking on a distinct sense of singularity.

Part One

The soul is large, expansive, and wise, so when making its plans, time and space do not limit it in creating different experiences. In the beginning of our journey as a soul, we spend time in the higher dimension as the huge soul we are. We create and experiment as the creators we also are.

Eventually, after millennia in the higher realm, some souls choose to come to Earth for the experience we have here. It's not an easy realm and we can get stuck in the energy cycle of Earth. But the soul knows what it wants to experience. As infinite souls, challenges and obstacles don't scare us because we understand that life on Earth is short and will be over in the blink of an eye. We know we can overcome the challenges, which is essential for our evolution. Unfortunately, humans have a limited frame of reference when viewing life's situations. We can become caught up in our thoughts, fears, and negative emotions.

As an infinite soul, you choose to work on some of the harrowing lives you've had. You want to bring healing gifts back into this life, but you know that the trauma and pain have blocked your talents, here and in other lives. So, as you make your plan, you pick a dozen lives where you were a gifted healer and actualized your gifts. Unfortunately, you also have a dozen lifetimes where you lost your life because you were a healer.

In this lifetime, you've studied healing and know you're talented, but you are afraid to advertise. You don't even want to tell your family for fear of their ridicule, which feels scary. Now that you've realized how extensive the fear is, you decide to identify where it is rooted to release. You want to create a successful business and not be afraid of showing up for your clients. You begin the work of uprooting its source.

When you learn to access your own Akashic Record, you can open the door to receiving true stories about who you have been. You can reclaim the wisdom from these lives and the talents you've had in them. If you were a healer in the 1500s, the townspeople might have killed you after deciding you were a witch—but you also would have tremendous talents to reclaim. You were a wise woman or man, an herbalist, and a doctor. You understood bones and could set a leg and save a person from gangrene with your herbs and poultices. This is information worth reclaiming—but first, you must clear and release the physical and emotional pain caused by your untimely and unfair death.

The idea is to move outside of the limitations of time and into the quantum field, where you can move around freely. You can zero in on the date given in the Akashic Record by focusing on one life at a time. Then you can go into the energy of that time and release the stuck energy by going outside of time and space.

Imagine the first thing you see as you go back in time is a cold and damp dungeon. We'd start by clearing the dark energy and fear from that moment. Then you see a torture room; there are layers of physical pain to remove emotional distress, trauma, and anxiety. Next, we go through the images, releasing the pain. We then energetically find the day the authorities burned you at the stake for being a witch. Many people are watching, both children and adults, including the person who told the authorities that you were a witch because she was jealous of your healing skills. You can see your husband and daughter crying, feeling betrayed and angry.

We go through each picture or image identifying the emotion still there and release it. Remember, these are old, stuck emotions holding you back in the present, impeding you from receiving the gifts from that life. It is essential to clear the physical pain, fear, anger, and betrayal. We also want to release any jealousy, even though it may belong to someone else. It would be stuck in your energy field as part of the betrayal. This process frees up who you were in that life and the skills you perfected. If you were a doctor and an herbalist, you can reclaim these gifts in this day and time.

We can picture this emotional pain as barbed wire wrapped around the wisdom and the gifts from that life, constricting them. When we release the barbed wire, we free the gifts and bring them into the present time in your body.

You can feel the quantum energy flowing through you and everything and everyone around you. The images change as we release all the unconscious memories left from the pain and trauma. This quantum field is a part of the Akasha.

The Akashic Record Keepers tell us that our futures are not engraved in stone. Everything is always fluid and changeable, which is excellent news, because we can go into what we perceive as a past-life trauma and alter it. When we do this type of Akashic quantum healing, we transform the past to change the present perception, energy, and experience.

You will likely experience a feeling of lightness and expansion from a quantum Akashic healing. Suddenly, you realize you are no longer afraid to tell your friends and family about your healing gifts, because you feel safe now.

CLEAR BLOCKS AND RECLAIM YOUR GIFTS AND TALENTS

Once we have cleared trauma, we are ready to reclaim the gifts stuck in the energy from the past. We may discover a few lifetimes that still affect our ability to fulfill our purposes in life. You might even feel the strong effects of a different past-life trauma. You might have had five or ten lifetimes like the one you had as a witch, which we cleared.

We would then go back into the quantum field through the Akasha, and you would envision the quantum energy as a vast spinning ball. We know there is no time in this field, so we ask the record keepers to help us zero in on another lifetime in which others harmed you because of your healing gifts. Once we've connected energetically with that life, we can go into the specific images to actively release the physical and emotional pain from this second life. The mystery to most of us is that we can still feel the fear, anger, and pain. Sometimes we can even remember a fragment of what happened, but we don't know where it came from and why it's haunting us.

Some people feel physical pain in their bodies from a knife or sword wound. This can create physical pain, which can be hard to fix because it's stuck outside of time and needs an energetic release. This is why Akashic quantum healing is so profound. We can go to that time, release the pain and trauma, reclaim the wisdom, and bring it into your body now.

MIND-BENDING AND PROFOUND

Once we have moved outside of the time/space continuum to heal trauma from the past, releasing blocks to reclaim needed information and memories we have from other lifetimes, our lives change, because we are no longer encumbered by what happened to us in our past lives.

We can only erase those karmic patterns where we have learned the lesson and moved on. If you still have things to learn, then the karma is still important to your soul. In a similar way, we can only unwrite or release stuck energy from some present-life contracts. If they truly are complete, the record keepers will tell us that so we can release them. Some patterns might still have purpose in your life and the life of the person you wrote the contract with, even if the circumstances feel uncomfortable. Yet, you can do considerable transformational work in your Akashic Record, including updating old contracts and energetically clearing areas in your life that no longer serve you.

SHIFT THE FUTURE

We can use the Akashic quantum field to go into the future and re-write information that we consciously or unconsciously put there. This can help us to unlock our ability to reach love and forgiveness.

Imagine when you were a small child with an idea or vision of romantic love. It might have come from a movie or a storybook. For example, you watched the story of Cinderella as a six-year-old. You loved the story of how Prince Charming came looking for Cinderella after the ball and finally found her. He rescued her from her evil stepfamily, and they lived happily ever after.

You, as a small child, want someone to rescue and care for you, and so you project this image and feeling out into your future. This energy of "Prince Charming" may block you from finding the person you have a soul contract with, because they don't fit the "Prince Charming" image. We can go into the Akashic Records to find the ideas and notions about the love you've projected into your future that no longer align with your highest path.

You might have had to take care of younger siblings as a child. You then vowed to never have a family and you sent that energy, unconsciously, out into the future. Now you want to have a family but find you can't find the right partner and you fear that you'll run out of time. It is time to ask your Akashic Record Keepers for help.

USING TIMELINES FOR HEALING

For many, it is easier to imagine the quantum field a timeline rather than a swirling ball of energy. In your mind's eye, picture a long ruler or some form of a linear timeline. Then, see yourself standing in the middle of the timeline, with lots of space to the left, which is the past, and plenty of room to the right, which is the future. When I say plenty of space, imagine you're standing on a train track in a flat desert landscape, and you can see miles to the left and to the right with the train track stretching out to the horizon in both directions.

As an example, let's do a simple exercise to clear the energy of "waiting for Prince Charming" or the perfect partner, so you can get on with life to find a loving soul partner. You climb aboard a handcart and begin pumping the handle, driving yourself forward until you see or feel the future picture of Prince Charming—the one you imagined long ago. Now you can invite Prince Charming to step up onto the handcart and roll in the other direction, taking him back to you standing on the train track.

Now invite the energy and idea of the princess to integrate into your energy body in the now, to reclaim any of the energy you projected out into the future. When you feel you are complete, you can resume pumping the hand cart toward the future again. You ask your record keepers to show you any thoughts, feelings, ideas, or pictures of the person you are meant to marry or be in a relationship with. Once you know where the images are, you can go directly to them to either release them or bring the energy back into the present time. This will remove old, stuck energy and reclaim it, so you can move forward unburdened by your old ideas.

Whether energy is stuck in the past or the future, you need to release it and transmute it into something you want to create. Remember that everything is energy, and energy is infinite, so we cannot destroy it. Instead, we transmute it by recycling the energy into its original, pure light form to manifest what we desire. By transmuting the energy, you can utilize it now rather than leaving it in the future, which would only limit your access in the present moment.

NOTHING IS WRITTEN IN STONE

As I mentioned, nothing was written in stone. You can relax knowing you preplanned your experiences to create a purposeful life of growth and service, but your decisions are still under your control. Even though the Akasha holds the recordings of all living things' past, present, and future knowledge, the future is not inevitable. Instead, it can change according to your choices, as we have free will.

The essential part of soul work is changing how we process deeply unconscious thoughts and emotions, which keep us locked in old patterns.

Part One

That's the magnificent reason the soul comes back so many times. In reincarnating, our physical life supports the soul's desire to find joy and love.

PATH TO AWAKENING

Many years ago, the record keepers told me that working in the Akasha is a path to awakening. I asked how that worked. They explained that we can move into a place of greater compassion, love, and forgiveness when we understand the bigger picture. Those vibrations move us into a higher state of awakening. As we walk the path of compassion and love, we can share those high vibrations with humanity, helping others as we build bridges toward awakening.

When we can master the world's challenges, overcome emotional pain and trauma, and move out of victimhood, our day-to-day life changes. We can begin doing the highest level of soul work by sharing our light and transforming the world. The record keepers remind me often that, as we heal ourselves, our healing ripples out into the world, helping others.

When we raise our vibration, we help others rise to match the higher frequency so they can heal. In the process, we build bridges into the fourth and fifth dimensions and onward. Our ability to change the energy from negative to positive through our choices makes us the bridge builders and lightworkers that we came here to be.

Having a more expanded view of our soul contracts, karmic patterns, and our purpose will help as we move forward. Also, when we realize that our struggles to transform old, stuck energy and turn it into a higher frequency of love and forgiveness help humanity and Earth's inhabitants, it makes it all worthwhile. I'm glad you are on this journey with me. The world needs your light.

I'm so excited for you to read the following stories as each writer shares their intimate relationship with their own Akasha to receive guidance, healing, ideas, and unconditional love on their journeys. I'm sure you will enjoy their stories and find similar events in your life.

PART TWO

Spiritual Experiences of Accessing the Infinite Intelligence of Our Souls

*You, yourself, as much as anybody in the entire universe,
deserve your love and affection.*

—BUDDHA

MY LIFE AS A WHALE

One of my most profound experiences in the Akashic Records happened almost twenty years ago. This was back in the day when I had a brick-and-mortar business.

I held weekend Akashic Records workshops with my Five-Step Wisdom Prayer System to teach students to quickly access their personal records. During the weekend, we had many practice exercises so that all the students got comfortable asking questions and receiving guidance from their Akashic Record Keepers.

One of the exercises I gave the students was to pull an oracle card and ask the Akashic Records to tell them a story about the card they just drew. I sometimes enjoyed joining the students in the exercises, because we always receive new information and more profound wisdom as we continue working in our own Akashic Records.

I had a beautiful Oracle deck with unusual, otherworldly art. As I walked around, holding out the deck of cards for each student to pick one, I talked about how we live hundreds and hundreds of lifetimes here on Earth, but thousands of lifetimes on other planets and dimensions.

Part Two

For this exercise, the Akashic Record Keepers suggested we do an exercise that included other worlds, times, or possible dimensions. So, after everyone had a card, I pulled one for myself. When each person opened their records, I instructed them to ask their record keepers to tell them the story of their life and the time the card represented. I did the same for myself.

The artwork on the card I chose showed a frozen landscape that stretched all the way to the edge of the ocean. Everything in the picture was barren—no trees or plants, only ice, snow, and water. When I asked my record keepers to tell me the story of my life when I lived in this frozen world, they said, *You came to Earth from Sirius, the Dog Star, as a whale. Sirius has two planets, known as A and B. The whales and dolphins came from Sirius A. Many souls came to Earth as whales and dolphins before humans inhabited Earth. They enjoyed the great and deep oceans of Earth. Other beings came to Egypt from the stars and eventually became known as the Egyptian gods and goddesses. They also came from Sirius B. There was a variety of life on Sirius B. Many types of beings, including lion beings with wings, feline-like beings, blue-skinned beings, and an elemental type of being.*

The record keepers also said that as a soul, I loved to travel galactically and often went to other worlds and planets. Then, over one hundred thousand years ago, I came to our beautiful Earth as a whale. I loved the pristine, crystal blue, ice cold water. I can see myself as a huge creature doing spirals through the water, swimming hundreds of miles to find the perfect food for me. There was infinite space to dive to great depths and to fly for a moment in the open air as I breached the water into the sky. There was wonderous life under the sea and little else living on this planet. I was so in love with Earth that I made a vow to the beautiful, sentient being that Gaia herself is: I vowed that I would always support her.

The record keepers told me I had made this vow 130,000 years ago. That piece was so fascinating and really gave my present life greater meaning. In my life now, I have often asked why I was back on Earth again. This experience gave me a different way of looking at my life and an unexpected answer to that question. At some point, when I was inquiring how many lives I'd lived, the record keepers told me that I've lived over one thousand lifetimes here on Earth. That is approximately 200 lifetimes more than the average soul!

I asked, "Was this because I was very slow in learning and completing karmic patterns?" I was a bit surprised when they replied it was because I came back, again and again, to be of service and assistance to Gaia and humanity. Vows are extraordinarily strong and affect our soul plan and our choices. I am an Earth guardian, helping Mother Earth to awaken and ascend.

I also knew that during the Golden Age of our world, many thousands of years ago, I made a vow to help humanity to remember and awaken. That is what I do now. I help humanity remember the greater truth of who they are as wise and infinite souls.

One of my contracts is to assist the record keepers in bringing Akasha's ancient wisdom back to the world at this time in history. But I have realized my reason for returning to Earth so many times was to learn and grow as a soul and to support humanity's growth. And finally, at this crucial time in history, I have returned to help awaken humanity through the Akasha.

I sat with that beautiful oracle card in my hands and realized my view of my life had just shifted. I would never think of myself or my life in the same way. My story from the record keepers validated that I was a powerful and infinite soul, here to help the awakening and the ascension.

I learned that I wasn't here because I still had much to learn. But because I had the gift of a connection with the Akashic Records, I could help people connect to this Divine wisdom. I help them to understand their soul's plan and receive validation of who they are, which is often life-changing.

Lisa Barnett

ANCESTRAL HEALING

'm not really sure how I injured my lower back. Maybe it was the gym, or maybe I held my three-year-old child on the same hip too many times, causing rotation in my lower lumbars.

With a family ski trip to Austria only two weeks away, I tried everything to help the constant pain in my back including chiropractic adjustments, acupuncture, and massage therapy. Nothing worked and I was in a tailspin, wondering where I could find relief.

At the same time, I was in the middle of uncovering yet another layer in my bioenergetics therapy sessions. I had been going to therapy twice a week: one session for me to unwind my childhood sexual abuse traumas, and a second that I attended with my husband for couples therapy.

My back pain became unbearable, as if I were reaching a crescendo. I called my therapist, crying in pain. "Mary, please help me! I can't ride on a plane for nine hours next week in this excruciating pain!"

Mary was angelic. She stood five-foot-one with deep-set brown eyes and a soft voice. "Of course, dear," she replied. "We can address this in your next session on Tuesday."

Part Two

Tuesday morning, I struggled to send the kids off to school with my stiff back, but knowing it was therapy day kept some hope alive. As I entered my therapist's office, her little Yorkie came running up to greet me. I couldn't deal with the pinching pain of bending over to pet the dog this morning. Mary has described her pet as a therapy dog who assists her clients. She said when people are finished emoting in the adult therapy gym, her dog will sit on the couch and help the client destress further by allowing them to pet her.

"Petting an animal is an act of love," she said. "Dopamine will eventually activate, which allows the body to calm down and resume homeostasis."

Mary carefully watched my thirty-four-year-old body shuffle in like a senior citizen. I walked as if I'd been in a car accident, minus the neck collar. I told her I didn't want to sit, so she pulled out a sawhorse with a pillow fastened on top. She told me to put my belly on top of the pillow and to bend over, to open up my vertebrae. I obliged, finally feeling some pressure release from the lack of gravity pressing into my spinous processes.

"Now what, Mary? I can't take this sawhorse with me on the plane," I joked.

"Breathe out loud. I want to hear your exhales with a sound," Mary said.

I took my first loud breath. Inhale. Exhale, "Ahhhhhhhhh."

"Again!" she instructed.

So, I inhaled. Then I exhaled, "Haaaaaaaaa!"

"Again!" she demanded. Mary's soft voice was starting to get a bit of a tone. "This time, close your eyes and FEEL into yor exhales!" she thundered.

I inhaled deeply and exhaled, "Aooooooooo!"

My eyes were closed, but my mind jumped into another reality. Suddenly, I saw myself running through an autumn forest in the dead of night.

"Can you hear those wolves?" I cried. "They're coming! They're after me!"

I wanted to open my eyes and climb back off the sawhorse, but Mary reassured me that I was safe. "Go back, back to where you were before you started running."

I took another inhale and an audible exhale. "I'm sitting in an old, dark, stony castle with my parents having dinner by candlelight in front of a huge, open hearth where the food is cooked. They are my parents today, as well. Except my father is huge, not five-foot-four like he is in this life. He seems at least six feet tall and heavy, like an ogre. My mother is a slight woman; she has a sharp jaw, a pointy chin, and darting eyes. Her hair has been pulled back in a plain, low bun." My mother's mousey, pale, boyish demeanor was a stark contrast to her voluptuousness of today.

"The plates and goblets are made of pewter," I continued. "My father is drunk and has food stains on his shirt. Grease and red wine drip from his bushy, red beard as he lustfully stares me down. My mother sits to my left and seems angry. My father is on my right side at the head of the table, raving like an intoxicated dictator and talking with his mouth full. I can see long, blond hair cascading down the front of my dark grey dress. My cold, pale hands are resting on my lap."

I described for my therapist how I excused myself to go to my room. Shortly afterwards, my father pushed open my door and tried to crawl up onto my bed. The bed was very high off the floor. In my terror, I felt a burst of adrenaline and, with new strength, I shoved him off the bed."

With a Celtic accent, I screamed, "No more! Not tonight! Not ever!"

In his drunkenness, he had fallen heavily to the stone floor, hitting his head. Blood slowly oozed from behind his fiery red hair. I hopped off the other side of my bed and ran out of the room and down a long corridor toward a back staircase. I was barefoot, wearing only a long, white, cotton nightgown. I spiraled down the cold, stone steps in the old turret, trying to glance out of the skinny window slits. When I reached the main floor, I grabbed a scratchy grey cloak from a wooden peg and bolted out the side door and ran into the woods.

"I keep glancing behind myself to make sure I'm not being followed," I said. "There's a bit of a river to cross. I'm so cold. I make it across the narrow

Part Two

part of the stream, leaping like a jackrabbit in pursuit of safety. I run deeper into the wooded forest that surrounds the castle. I can barely feel my naked feet starting to freeze. And now I hear the sounds of the wolves crying 'Aooooooo!' into the unforgiving, dead, frigid Irish air."

I told my therapist of wrapping the cloak around me to keep warm and to hide, shaking, my heart pounding. After a little while, I stopped feeling cold and noticed myself rising from the forest, out of my body.

"No, no, no! It's not right! It's not fair! No, no, no!" I cried. I screamed and cursed in Celtic.

"What year is it?" Mary asked.

"1576!"

"Move forward, dear," she instructed. "Where are you now?"

I took another deep breath and suddenly saw a wooden box being carried with a single processional line following, plus one bagpiper. They were walking to a family plot on the castle grounds where past loved ones were laid to rest. I was hovering over my mother's head like a little bird, listening to her friend say, "Well, it's just as well. She was mad. She told the vicar your husband was raping her!"

"My mother pursed her thin lips a little tighter and said nothing, staring into the distance," I said.

"I want you to climb down off the sawhorse and sit on the carpeted floor," Mary said. She handed me a glass of water. I scooted over to rest my back against the couch.

"Wow, I feel like my whole thoracic body is hollow," I exclaimed. I put one hand on my chest and another on my belly. "I feel empty in here... is that normal?"

I took a sip of water. Mary's little dog trotted around the corner and plopped down on my thigh, looking up at me expectantly. I started to pet her while Mary explained that she had only seen this happen twice in her thirty years of counseling.

"It's not uncommon to have a past-life entity move through a person while uncovering severe trauma," she said matter-of-factly. "We often incarnate within our family tree lines in order to keep working through our themes and patterns of abuse."

"Oh my God, is that what just happened? That abused Irish girl from the castle was me?"

Mary nodded her head. "Most likely, yes."

We both smelled a strong rose fragrance. "Do you smell anything?" she asked.

"Yes," I said as I witnessed an apparition of a young woman with long, blond hair standing in a white nightgown, handing me yellow roses.

"Mmmmary, do you see her too?" I asked in disbelief.

"No, I don't see anything, dear."

The apparition of a past-life version of me stood in front of me, pointing toward my belly button. She said in an Irish accent, "Thank you for releasing me. I was living here…"

I realized she was pointing through my belly to the anterior aspect of my third lumbar vertebra as she added, "Now I am free to help you heal from your sexual abuse."

"What's happening?" I cried in disbelief.

Mary reassured me that all was well, but I felt unsettled after seeing my own ghost. I explained that, as a chiropractor, my husband often had to adjust my L-3, which enervates the sexual organs. He had revealed that some of his patients who have shared their sexual abuse stories with him also had L-3 issues.

I got up off the floor without any pain. Within an hour, my old-lady shuffle was completely gone. I felt as though I was released from something holding me down, and yet I still felt open. The strange, hollow sensation lingered. When it was time to leave, I stood up straight. I found I could even bend over to pet her little doggie good-bye without any moans or groans.

Part Two

Mary explained that bioenergetics can help us release our tiny boxes of unfelt emotional pain that have become stuck within the body. This unfelt pain can cause discomfort and disease. In this case, pain had been stuck in my ancestral lineage, which I had carried into this life to be healed.

As an intuitive, I've studied the Akashic Field. Our Akashic Records are like a library of every incarnation our soul embodies. It sometimes takes a soul many lifetimes to complete a theme. We are being tasked to resolve the past abuses of our lineage while we are present at this time in our Earth's evolution. My past incarnation had come to help me release the generational bondage that had marred my family tree for centuries.

Fifteen years later, my husband and I were invited to attend the grand opening of a boutique hotel at a castle in Ireland. We were thrilled to visit Ireland to trace my Irish roots, and of course, to stay in a castle. My ancestors had been horse breeders in Kilkenny, which is the town next to Castle Kilkea. We rented a car in Dublin and drove an hour to the castle.

Driving down the long, heavily wooded driveway toward the castle in autumn felt eerily familiar. When we arrived at the castle's main entrance, I looked up at the plain, grey structure and experienced a moment of *deja vu*. We were given a tour, during which I was able to investigate the turret at the far end of the castle, which had been used by the kitchen staff. I felt compelled to climb those stairs rather than the main staircase.

I've been here before, I thought, as goosebumps rose on the back of my neck. The turret staircase was illuminated by tall, skinny window slits. The castle, which was built in 1180, is now surrounded by an eighteen-hole golf course. From the roof, I had a good view of the whole property. I could see a river that surrounded the castle like a mote. I asked what was here before the golf greens and the caretaker said, "Just heavily wooded land.

We were assigned a lovely room on the second floor, overlooking the rose gardens below. After unpacking, I strolled around the grounds and ended up at the castle grave site. A black, wrought-iron gate guarded the entrance to the past loved ones laid to rest. The stones were too old for me to read the etchings, but I felt a remembrance of sorts.

The circle is now complete. I have released the tormented Irish girl who lived within the ancestry of my bones. Through the Akashic Field, we had healed generations of abuse. Our lineage was set free.

Michelle McClennen

PAINTING THE AKASHA

With a broad sweep of my arm, I dash a swath of deep magenta paint across the canvas. Ribbons of color crisscross in organic shapes. I feel captivated by the flow of paint, the movement of the arm, hand, and brush as one. A vibration of energy pours through me. It flows into my hand, guiding the brush. I liquefy the paint, allowing it to drip and flow. The color shimmers. The canvas fills with curvilinear shapes, a visual representation of the energy moving through me. I'm excited to begin a new piece of art.

I step back to survey the painting and perch on my stool. As I observe my work, I become introspective. Suddenly, I'm aware of being in an altered state of time and space. I smell the musky dampness of a dark-paneled room. I sense myself standing in front of an easel that holds a painting.

It's a portrait of a woman. Her skin is porcelain white, her dress a deep, maroon red with long billowy sleeves. The colors blend in a smoky, atmospheric effect. The walnut brown background glows as the oil paint reflects the light. I hold a long-handled brush. As I paint, it glides across the wooden panel, each stroke blending into the next. I add yellow ochre

Part Two

to emphasize the effect of light. Flaked white paint adds highlights to the woman's neck and face.

Painting portraits is my passion. I sense the woman's emotions by the way she tilts her head, folds her hands, and looks past me. I ask God for Divine guidance in expressing what she feels and the essence of her stoic character, her social status, her beauty, and her opulent dress.

The vision vanishes. I realize I'm in my studio, staring out the window but seeing nothing. I recognize that I had been experiencing another lifetime. I have intuitively accessed my Akashic Records: the records of my soul. I've experienced my records before, but never so vividly.

I'm exhilarated. A pulling sensation surrounds my heart. I sense one of my spirit guides behind my left shoulder. The message: *Being an artist is your soul's journey.*

Why did I doubt it? Painting feels natural to me. Now I know I've been an artist before. Gratitude overtakes me as tears form in my eyes. I feel surrounded by golden light.

I return to my painting, eager to access the Akashic Records again. They hold the story of my soul's journey from individuation from Source until it finally returns. I close my eyes and focus on my breath. I ask for guidance as I drift into stillness.

As an abstract artist, I rely on intuition and inner vision when I paint. I open my eyes and pick up the brush. My hand is drawn to the colors: sap green, turquoise, and deep blue. They blend into a subtle, gray-green turquoise. I brush it across the canvas in a series of undulating lines. The color harmonizes with the magenta. I add areas of deep yellow ochre. Rippling shapes fill the canvas.

Vibratory energy directs my brushstrokes and the rhythm and flow of the paint. I don't know yet what the subject matter is. It evolves with the work. I hear with my inner ears, *Just let go. You've done this before. Trust!*

I had learned to enter the Akashic Records with prayers containing symbolic and vibratory keys. The prayers start and end my creative process. This raises my vibration, so the elements of art such as balance, proportion, harmony, and rhythm merge seamlessly with my creativity. I'm energized to retrieve the Akashic "information library" of my soul that connects to the vibration and purpose of the painting. I allow myself to be led by spiritual force, which has innate intelligence. I'm its conduit. As spirit moves through me, I allow the painting to unfold with the Akashic wisdom guiding me.

Now I'm ready to complete my work in progress. I relax, ground myself energetically, and read the opening prayer. I sense a connection with my Akashic masters, teachers, and beings of light. I feel my heart expand and fill with love. The energy swells, lifting me into a higher vibratory plane.

Instinctively, I pick up the brush with my non-dominant hand and mix a dab of lemon yellow with ochre. I swirl the brush on the canvas in uncontrolled strokes that morph into golden clouds.

My breathing slows. The energy softens and I move the brush gently. Brushstrokes of magenta form twin hearts lifting out of the gold. Below it, a cityscape appears with a series of vertical turquoise lines. More heart shapes form as the gold and blue areas intertwine. When the meditative state subsides, I return to normal consciousness.

I evaluate the painting to see how the eye is led through it. With a blue-green crayon and guidance from the Akasha, I sketch the major shapes and movement across the canvas, forming them into a cohesive whole. The work is complete. It's about unconditional love and opening the heart, expressed through abstract symbols retrieved from my Akashic Records. Since abstract art often represents the spiritual, this is a visual depiction of the transcendent power of love.

As the energy wanes, I bow my head and say the closing prayer. I thank the masters, and teachers of the Akashic Records for their unconditional love and ask them to close my records and return me to my human sensitivities.

Part Two

I ground myself into Mother Earth with energetic cords, sensing the outflow of energy.

I'm grateful I was able to harness the wisdom of the Akasha into art that expresses the sacredness of love.

Sheryl A. Stradling

STANDING OUT

Water rushes over my body. I feel its cool caress flowing through my fingers and past my toes. I see the billowy white clouds against a crystal blue backdrop of the sky. A sense of resounding peace fills my heart, mind, and body.

I hear a message: *You are a clear and perfect channel. In the realm of Spirit, you are free.*

I sensed the water washing away decades of anger, knowing that it was time to let it go. I was conscious of being in a quantum field of healing where anger and judgment transformed into acceptance and forgiveness.

As I grounded my body and slowly began to wiggle my toes and fingers, to become present in my body on this Earth, I knew I had been given a wonderful gift. My heart filled with peace and wonderment, as it had during my first guided meditation, more than twenty years ago.

During my journey with the Akasha and the spiritual realm, I have always been drawn to the healing modalities. Fiery energy emits from my hands as a solid pillar of light engulfs my physical body. An intense buzzing pulsation of protection fills me; it is the intensity of Spirit pouring into my head from my pineal gland outwards. I feel this intensity with every healing session I

Part Two

administer. Yet for the client, it feels like a peaceful slumber wrapped in the warmth of a cozy blanket.

I know that I give each client comfort and healing for issues that no longer serve them. Yet self-doubt sometimes creeps in. The ego, my parents, the friends who do not understand what I believe or what I do make me question myself. They tell me this is a nice hobby, but I'll never find clients, make money, or be a teacher.

"Go get a job," they advise.

If I believe them for an instant, my journey slows down. I do not tell people what I do. I haven't created business cards or flyers to tell people who I am. When I doubt myself, it makes my business, my dreams, and my ability to help people become stagnant. However, I have always felt this pull in my soul.

As the flowing water moves through me, I know it is time to declare who I am.

In a whispered voice, I hear, *Stand out.*

My body is numb. I hear myself ask, "Yes, but how?"

I hear no response, but I know Spirit's answer can show up in many different forms. I can only continue with my day.

I dreamed that same evening of a beautiful woman whose face and clothes appeared in orange and sepia tones. She asked me, *If you could choose from the following, which would you want? An accounting job or to stay in the muck? Don't think, just give me an answer.*

"Muck," I replied.

Then tell me, what do you want to do? As she asked, her image faded out of view.

A quiet space opened in my mind. I saw a clear and beautiful day. When I opened my back door, I could smell the salt water of the ocean. I could hear the waves crashing on the rocks below. It was peaceful and I was safe.

In the stillness, I knew that today I would meet new people who were intrigued and excited to learn about the Akasha. I would be their teacher and consultant. I am at peace with being the leader, for I have played this role in many lifetimes. I have lived as a shaman, a priest, a schoolteacher, and a mother who taught her children to be good people. I have all these roles within me.

That realization made a bell go off in my head. All those roles required me to stand out and be free from anyone else's perception of how or who I should be. My morning vision of rushing water had transformed me. I knew that I had moved into a place of acceptance and peace.

I asked my Akashic Record Keepers about this vision. They replied, *When you stand in your power, you are strong. There is no doubt, for everything falls into place. Just as this day will fall into place. See your heart radiating beautiful angelic and crystal energies in harmony with the elementals. They are your song. They are your Divine guidance, the angels and the elementals who assist you in this lifetime. This is your strength and your love. Like a Pied Piper, the people will find you. Just play and be who you are meant to be, the beautiful, Divine one that you are. Go play, little one, go play.*

With the support of my Akashic Record Keepers, I knew I was ready to live in peace and wonder for the rest of my life. I became ready to stand out.

Rebeka Lopez

MY ROAD TO FREEDOM

A small holding of land had been in my family for generations. It was in an idyllic setting in the countryside with views of the lakes and mountains on all sides. When I inherited the land from my father, it seemed only natural to build our home there. It would be a wonderful place to raise a family.

I had been a Reiki master for many years and I had friends who also worked as energy healers for the land. I asked them to check out the property, energetically, before we started building; when all had come up clear, I was happy to proceed. Over the next two years, we built a beautiful house and planted orchards and extensive gardens, as this was to be our home for life.

But shortly after moving in, both my health and that of my children began to deteriorate. None of us responded to medical treatment. It became clear that strong energy influences were at play in the house and on the land.

We had made a significant investment in the house. It seemed crazy to walk away with no real understanding of why this was happening. I energetically gridded the house to protect us as best as I knew how at that stage. Over the next couple of years, I invited numerous energy healers from all over the world to look at the property and carry out healings on the house

Part Two

and land. They were able to tell me what was energetically going on in the property, which verified what I was seeing and experiencing. Unfortunately, their healing work only held for a few days at a time.

Eventually, our health was being impacted so much that we decided to sell the property. The real estate agents were optimistic and we had lots of interest and viewings, but no firm offers. After a year had passed with no sign of the house selling, we moved to another house closer to where my husband worked. Within a matter of weeks, our health started to improve. We were still struggling but we did our best to move forward with our lives.

Three more years passed and the property still had not sold. I was beginning to lose hope. I felt deeply that this situation was connected to family karma on the land, so I began doing research into the ancient history of the area. I discovered there had been warring tribes there for hundreds of years.

One day, out of the blue, an old friend I hadn't seen for almost ten years contacted me. I met him and his wife that same day and we both immediately felt a sense of relief. He told me that he had been searching for me on the internet since I had moved away but wasn't able to find me. It was his wife who had finally tracked me down online.

My friend said he had felt that I was in some sort of trouble and needed his help, but he had no details for me. While talking with each other, we could see each other's faces morphing into other people, like photos flickering in front of our eyes. I told them about the situation with the land and the house and, as he and his wife were members of a Christian church, they said they would ask for prayers for the situation. I was grateful.

That night, I became sure there was a deep, karmic, past-life connection between my friend and I. Bright light surrounded me, an expansion in my energy field that I hadn't felt in years. A spark of hope and excitement had been ignited in my heart again, and I felt giddy, like a child. I knew he was a key to this situation.

Before bed, I went into meditation and called in a column of Christ-conscious light to come down through and around me. Then I asked to be shown why this friend was back in my life. I immediately lost conscious awareness of my physical body and, within seconds, I observed that I was in a large, white room. This room was the shape of a cathedral but on a much grander scale than anything I had ever seen on Earth. There was an atmosphere of bliss that felt like a warm blanket being wrapped around me. I was completely cocooned in love as my body became one with the light. In a state of pure bliss and pure love, with no awareness of time, I just was.

The next moment, I could sense light beings coming toward me on every side. They were completely luminescent. I felt the most incredible love from them, as if they were my family. I could feel the embrace of their energy within mine. One of them reached out and a blue sphere of light began to materialize in front of me. It became a movie screen where I was shown that my friend and I had lived numerous lifetimes together. Then they showed me, in vivid detail, a lifetime where we had been connected on the land where my former house stood.

My friend and I had been leaders of warring tribes. A great betrayal between both sides had taken place exactly on the spot where my husband and I had built our house. They said the area had been sealed off by the Land Guardians generations before this lifetime, to bring about peace. That is why the other energy healers and I had been unable to pick up the negative energy portal that was present before we started to build. The beings said that, by breaking ground on the land to install the foundations of the house, we had reopened a portal to that warring time.

It was as if my family had been living in a battlefield.

They told me that I held the keys and codes to shut down that portal. This was why my father had passed this land down to me, rather than giving it to another sibling. This was why other healers had been unsuccessful at permanently closing this portal. They said I was the only one who could accomplish this.

In that moment, everything suddenly made sense. All the human suffering we had endured in that house and on that land wasn't in vain. There had been a greater reason.

I was to walk that property, together with my friend, with the intention of restoring peace and shutting down that portal. Once the light beings gifted me with this knowledge, they started to work within my energy field to prepare me for the task ahead. Ribbons of light, of every color and shade, moved around me, forming a spinning top with a diamond white center. The beings said they were going to remove shadow elements in my field and reactivate codes and sacred geometry that had been dormant within me. I had the awareness of my energy body being pivoted from side to side and up and down.

The ribbons of light started to fade into the background until I couldn't see them anymore. I was to rest while I integrated this new frequency within my field. I felt so blessed, so grateful and privileged to have received this activation and healing. I thanked these beautiful beings for their teaching and blessing. As they began to fade into the background, I felt myself coming back into my physical body. Tears of joy and elation consumed me. I was aware that a great healing had taken place. If I could follow the guidance I had been given, our liberation was in sight.

I arranged to travel to the property, with my friend and his wife, the following week. My family of light had prepared us for the work that I hoped would bring a final resolution to this situation.

On the journey there, fear begin to rise within me. Memories of the energies that I had experienced while I lived there came to the surface. However, once we arrived at the property, my intuition took over. I knew exactly where to go and what to do. We walked the perimeter as the friends we are in this lifetime, knowing that we were surrendering, forgiving, and healing the past and bringing peace to the present. As we did so, I felt a shift in the energy on the property. I knew the healing was working on all levels now.

Within three weeks, we had a secure offer on the house. That same week, my family of light visited me again in a vivid dream and told me I had to gift the land along with the house, as a way of relinquishing the past completely. Elation rose within me as I felt peace return to our lives. My children and I began to sleep through the night and for extended periods during the day as our bodies healed. The light that we received as a family, from that moment on, was incredible and I will be forever grateful.

As soon as the sale of the house was agreed upon, I was guided to leave that country and start afresh somewhere else. My friend and his wife accompanied us to the ferry port and we headed away. But at the very moment that we parted, a second piece of the karmic connection with my friend arose. We both felt the most incredible pain in every part of our bodies at having been physically separated. It was as if we were conjoined twins being ripped apart. This physical and emotional pain subsided over a couple of days, but the energetic connection between us grew stronger, despite living in different countries now.

Our relationship had always been purely platonic. He had always felt like a brother to me. Now we spoke on the phone every day. The energy between us became increasingly consuming. Neither of us could understand what was going on. It began to interfere with our day-to-day lives.

I went online and found some information about breaking vows from past lives through the Akashic Records. While studying reiki, I had learned about breaking vows of chastity, poverty, and obedience. *Were there other past-life vows influencing my present lifetime?*

I went into a deep state of meditation again and, as before, I was taken up into the white cathedral of light. I was shown two more lifetimes with my friend where we had been romantically connected and had been separated

Part Two

through war and through early death. In our last lifetime together, we had made a vow of undying love for each other.

As soon as I was aware of this, I was able to release this vow. I physically felt the release from my body, as if someone had pulled a plug out of an electrical socket. The energies and feelings between my friend and I were released immediately. Initially, I didn't tell him what I had discovered and the steps I had taken to break our vow, but when I didn't hear from him for more than a week, I knew it had worked. When we spoke again, he told me that he didn't know what had happened, but the energy between us had somehow subsided. We were able to move on with our separate lives.

Siobhan Maguire

PIUS MARTIN

The melodic voice, soothing and familiar, flowed from the small, tabletop player beside my bed. I was approaching the deep alpha state of my Akashic meditation when I heard a man's voice—not through my ears, but in my forehead.

The voice said, in a voice soft and low, *Pius Martin.*

My eyes flew open and I sat up in bed, astonished by the voice I had so clearly heard. I knew the voice and name were not part of my routine meditational recording, so I pointed the remote control at the player and set it on pause. Remaining perfectly still, I strained my ears and listened, but heard only the familiar sounds of a household at rest for the night.

Could I have imagined the voice? Lying back upon my pillow, I once again felt my body relax as I closed my eyes. But before I could resume the recording, I heard the voice ring out again, loud and clear: *Pius Martin!*

I knew without a doubt that I had heard a man's voice—again, not through my ears, but in my head. Silently, I mouthed the name Pius Martin over and over. *Who on Earth is this man?* I could think of no one by that name, nor could I come to any immediate conclusions about who he might be.

Part Two

Once more, I laid back and closed my eyes. This time, I saw him in a vision that played out like a movie behind my closed eyelids. The man was dressed in a brown robe tied at the waist by a cream-colored length of rope. What appeared to be a hood hung loosely about his neck. As he walked toward me, I noticed sandals adorning his feet although they were barely visible below the hem of the robe that swished about his legs. His arms slowly opened and extended toward me. I could see the kindness in his eyes and his sweet smile.

His lips moved, and once again I heard *Pius Martin*. Then the vision faded. A soothing, peaceful feeling swept over me, and I drifted into a deep sleep.

When the morning light streamed into my bedroom through the leaded glass window, so bright and vibrant that it almost hurt my eyes, I lay still for a moment, soaking up its warmth on my face. Slowly, very slowly, I opened my eyes. I sat up and marveled at the circles the sunlight wove onto the hardwood floor. I was musing over the way the light was refracted by the heavy, lead glass when I suddenly remembered the name I'd heard so clearly the night before: *Pius Martin*.

I quickly made my way across the room to the computer and typed in the name. A deep, inner joy and peace filled me, as though I had been given a special gift. And indeed, that is what had happened! My research revealed that an Irish American by the name of Bill Martin had nursed Padre Pio during the final three years of his life.

Padre Pio was one of the most famous healers and beloved saints of the 20th century. He was a Capuchin priest who carried the stigmata—the appearance of bodily wounds, scars, and pain in locations corresponding to the crucifixion wounds of Jesus Christ—on his hands, wrists, and feet. Padre Pio also had the ability of bilocation and prophecy. He was able to read souls. Following Padre Pio's death in 1968, Bill Martin became ordained as a Capuchin priest; thereafter, he was called Father Joseph Pius Martin.

Father Joseph spent the rest of his life in San Giovanni Rotondo, Italy making the padre known to the world. He assisted thousands of pilgrims who visited Padre Pio's tomb over the years.

I could not believe my eyes. There in print was the name I had clearly heard! I sat in stunned silence wondering what to make of this revelation.

As a young child, I'd had a strong connection to animals and nature. By the age of seven, I demonstrated an uncanny ability to heal sick and injured animals. I could also manifest energy from my hands into unhealthy and dying plants, bringing them back to a healthy state. Even at that young age, I knew about an ancient wisdom. It was real, yet indescribable from a child's perspective.

As I grew into a young adult, I became more and more aware of my healing abilities, and so I looked beyond traditional religious beliefs and began a life dedicated to the quest for spiritual enlightenment. I soon found that the path to enlightenment is neither easy nor straightforward. The path bends and turns and takes the seeker down many avenues of exploration until, one day, the way forward becomes crystal clear. After circumnavigating the world of mystical phenomena, I landed once again on the shores of noēsis and fully accepted my Creator-given gift of healing, the primary substance of my soul; my Akasha.

Vowing to explore that gift as fully and completely as possible, I began to study healing as an art. I turned to my ancient wisdom keepers, the feminine ancestors from whom my healing abilities flowed, and asked for guidance in manifesting this gift for the good of others, without benefit to myself. I soon found pathways opening that led me to like-minded people who assisted me in developing my art.

The path was not an easy one, requiring years of study. But over time, I became adept in sourcing my energy into a tangible resource benefiting the health of people, animals, and plants. I regularly practiced prayer and meditation to keep my spiritual connection and relationship to the

Part Two

Creator open. I continued to work at shaping my life as a healer, gradually accomplishing that goal one step at time.

But then, as it sometimes happens, life got in the way. My professional career began to skyrocket and work-related obligations increasingly took precedence over my soul's career. I found myself struggling to maintain the balance between my metaphysical and physical worlds. Unfortunately, the physical appeared to be winning. My career required that I travel throughout the country; for the next six years, I spent half my time on airplanes and in hotels.

Travel took a toll on my health. I experienced respiratory and immune-related illnesses that eventually required a twelve-month medical leave from my job. Knowing all too well the root cause of my illness or dis-ease, I was determined to make my way back to full health. I took advantage of the leave to rest, eat properly, and exercise. Soon, I began to heal physically. Then it was time for a full reassessment of my spiritual goals. I reconnected to the ancient knowledge I'd first realized in childhood and returned to my path of enlightenment through prayer and meditation. Over time, I felt a shift in my consciousness that told me I was on the road to spiritual healing.

I resumed my professional career, but asked that my job description include no travel and no long hours in the office. My requests were granted. I was a much happier employee. My colleagues often questioned my newfound joy in work and life; I chalked it up to the twelve-month leave of absence and explained that the time away had given me the rare opportunity to both regain my physical health and to reevaluate my soul's priorities.

New pathways opened for me professionally. I became involved with a group of doctors in the field of complementary and alternative medicine (CAM), moving away from traditional medical research and realigning my professional career. CAM provided healing touch as a medical modality for inpatient therapy; I was offered the opportunity to become trained and certified as a healing touch practitioner and I achieved a Level IV certification.

It was during this time that I first practiced the Akashic meditation that introduced me to Pius Martin. Although my initial reaction had been stunned silence, I soon realized that Father Joseph was communicating to me his approval, as well as that of Padre Pio. At that moment, I knew I was on the right path. Each day, I find affirmation and comfort in that knowledge.

Pamela Nance

THE AKASHIC STONE

Oscar Miro-Quesada, a well-known Peruvian-American curandero, and I met thirty years ago, each on a walk in a North Carolina forest. He was doing ceremony at the time and took me back to his lodge to share a mesa ceremony with me.

Years later, I was traveling with my son and daughter to celebrate their recent high school graduations. We were taking three weeks to slowly drive and hike The Grand Circle—a well-known itinerary crisscrossing the national parks and monuments of the southwestern United States.

As I slept in the little cabins behind the large hotel at Grand Canyon North, I was awakened by an apparition of a man with an ancient-looking face. Behind him was not the background of the room I was in, but a vast array of stars. He communicated telepathically.

He said, *I am a lineage amalgam. I am not a historical person. I represent a people who have long vanished. We know of your friend don Oscar's work and we want to be represented on his mesa—represented in his work.*

He paused before he spoke again, as if giving me time to take that in before he continued. *The next person who will come to you is a historical*

Part Two

person—but a historical person who is now passed. Watch for him. And then the apparition was gone.

The next night, in the same room, though I didn't expect it, I saw another appearance. This time, it was a male figure who appeared to be some kind of elder or chief. As he "presented himself," I clearly remembered the night before. I understood that he was about to give me directions related to the message I'd heard then.

His words were like a riddle. *Go to the staircase. Look for the wall that is white with a red splash—not striped as most—but with the prominent red splash. You will see it. There you will find a cave. At the cave, reach under, and take a stone. You will find it—one side red, one side white. Take it to your friend. This stone will represent my people.*

The next morning, I mentioned this to my kids. Reciting the words to them, I conjectured, "I guess 'the staircase' is The Grand Staircase Escalante. It appears I need to go to the Grand Staircase and look for a specific place, with a cave, where I will find a particular stone."

And then, being a good sport about all this stuff, I jokingly said to my kids, "Well, I guess we'll find out how crazy Dad really is."

Two days later, we hiked the river canyon in Zion National Park and the canyon trails of Bryce National Park. The Grand Staircase was next. I told my kids I was going to have to take this seriously and be on the lookout for the landmark the second apparition had described.

We were soon driving the Scenic Byway 12 that runs from Bryce Canyon to Grand Staircase Escalante and then up to Anasazi State Park. This region features grand and famous, red-and-white, striated sandstone formations known, both geologically and locally, as "hoodoos" or "zebra stripes." Along both sides of the road, there are precipitous drop-offs and occasional pullouts—called "waysides"—which most often include trailheads. Eventually, you top out at Head of the Rocks Overlook, a plateau-like area with several waysides and trailheads.

As we passed this overlook, I began to see cliffs off to the left where it appeared that the red and white sandstone was indeed less striped and had more splashes of red. Past the overlook, I began slowing down and looking far more carefully—especially to the left—in case I felt further prompted to pull off somewhere for more investigation. I found a flat area to park, marked with the characteristic sign at all trailheads: "Primitive Trail Beyond This Point, Follow Rock Markers."

Since there was plenty of scenery to see, I told the kids to enjoy walking around and that I would venture out—toward that row of cliffs that seemed more splashed with red than striped with red and white.

I had to go off-path to reach a white-faced cliff that appeared to have a prominent splash of red across it. *Am I crazy?* I wondered. By this time, I was far off the trail and beyond the markers noted by the warning signs, but I could still see both the cliff and the general area where I had parked the car. I felt confident I was not going to get lost.

Approaching the face of the cliff, I saw what appeared to be shadows along its base. *Could this be harbinger of a cave?*

I was surprised when I reached the cliff face. This was certainly not how I had imagined a cave! This opening in the rock was long and low, stretching left and right for many yards, but no more than a foot to a foot and a half in height. The entrance was wedged deeply into the cliff face, creating the long shadow I had seen from a distance.

Finally, the words of the second apparition—*reach under*—suddenly meant something. To explore this at all, I was going to have to reach into the darkness.

Now, because I'd been a plains-prairie kid who had a spent a lot of my younger years in rattlesnake country, I was not about to cavalierly plunge my hand into an opening in a rock. My mind also danced around with analyses:

Part Two

What has just happened here? Am I in the right place? But I then settled a little, comforted that at least everything that had just transpired made sense.

Breaking off a branch of nearby sagebrush, I probed about in the long, narrow darkness, careful to not disturb anything in the cave that might need to remain intact. Confident I'd been careful enough, and noting that I stood where the cave was at maximum height, the words spoken by the second apparition re-occurred to me: *Reach under and take a stone.*

I reached in and, in the dark, felt an assortment of stones. I grasped one and pulled it out. I was holding a stone that was white on one side and red on the other.

When these kinds of things happen in my life, I tend to "pick them up and then put them down" without analyzing too much afterwards. Accordingly, I mailed the stone to don Oscar and he reverently included it in his mesa work.

It is only now, seventeen years later, that my research—prompted by my writing of this piece—has turned up fascinating aspects of this story that I was completely unaware of at the time.

The location of this odd cave is about ten miles down road from Anasazi State Park. Along that road run the canyonlands once inhabited by the Anasazis. The small plateau at Head of the Rocks Overlook is perched directly above four now-well-known sets of ancient petroglyphs. There are four different glyph panels—the "Shaman and the Hunter," the "Alcove," the "100 Hands," and the "Bighorn." All can be reached directly from the Escalante River Trailhead, which stretches far below the Head of the Rocks Overlook area.

The ancient peoples often celebrated their ceremonies on the high places that overlooked this land. They left offerings and even buried their dead in these places. It is certainly possible that this location might have been such a ceremonial site.

I am grateful that the "Akashic Stone," which I found here by following the instructions of disincarnate visitors, continues to represent these ancient people.

Dr. Kurt Johnson

SEA OF LIFE

*F*or many years, I heard the Akashic Masters lovingly and patiently coax me to love myself: both the person I have grown into and the one I'd been in the past. Little by little, I had to learn what loving myself meant.

"What is wrong with me? What is going on inside of me? I feel something is broken," I would cry. "Am I am broken?"

Dear Heart, it is time for you to allow the breakdown of how you view your life and the reality of your choices to control yourself and others, the Akashic Masters would reply.

You are trying to make sense of your choices and how to make them fit into the place you put them all these years. They do not fit any longer. They are the past. You are not that person. We know when you make new choices, it creates a lot of resistance to change and challenges you to trust yourself. Even so, you must know your heart leads your beautiful life. Breathe into the truth of who you are as a light being filled with love for others. Now you must feel that way about yourself.

I had no idea how much my life would change when I opened myself to feeling and living with an open heart. I had been looking for a quick fix

Part Two

to making my life feel better. As I learned to trust the Akashic Masters and myself, I often felt like I was standing, with shaking knees, before the path of self-knowledge and self-love. Finally, I closed my eyes and walked forward.

This was my way out of a lifelong relationship with my pit of despair. For years, even as I started to have a firm footing on my path to loving myself, I would plunge—quickly and without notice—into that pit. I found myself trying to claw my way out of that dark, cold, scary place. But I never could.

The Akashic Masters were my mentors, always available to impart their wisdom and unconditional love. But it wasn't easy to let go of fear when I was filled with shame and guilt.

The "quick fix" involved continuous adjustments to my mental, emotional, physical, and spiritual levels of being. I guess my definition of quick isn't the same as my mentors'. Twenty-five-plus years of my life was possibly the blink of an eye to them.

I often lean on the Akashic Masters when I come to an impasse in my life and business. Recently, I began to feel my pit of despair open a chasm for me to fall through again. My desire to help others was somehow lost, replaced by my old fears and my shame.

How could I be so selfish? I asked. But beating myself up only made it worse. I knew somehow that the plan I had laid out was not aligned with my heart. Fighting my fear that the old pit would pull me in, I went to my long-time mentors for guidance.

"What has died in me?" I asked. "I feel no passion or drive to move forward."

With love and firmness, they shared: *Guilt, shame, and responsibilities for others didn't die in you. Instead, it shifted.*

I threw up my arms like a spoiled child who hadn't heard what she'd wanted to. "What is that supposed to mean?"

Patiently, they replied: *You are transitioning, learning to pull yourself away from being entangled with the needs of others so you can discover your own needs.*

"I still don't understand," I told them in an impatient voice. "I need examples."

Remember when you talked to your sister about the sinking feeling that was stealing your joy? You told her you couldn't find the source. You said that nothing was going on in your life or business to cause such a feeling.

"Yes, I remember."

Let us reframe it for you. You were not sinking; remember, your pit is gone. Rather, you were wading in the water without holding onto a life preserver. Your family and us. You were just with… you. All by yourself. It wasn't a feeling of sinking; it was a feeling of drifting. The drifting happens when your definition of who you are and what you mean to yourself and others becomes fractured. Your old story, the life preserver that had defined you, has dissolved.

Beginning that day, I decided to stand tall in my new story about who I am and how I got here. I also learned that when it's time to shift and grow, I might feel myself drift in the water—and that's a good thing.

It's so freeing to know that I no longer need to fear sinking into my pit of despair. I am simply drifting and wading in the sea of my life.

My relationship with the Akashic Masters sustain me. I have built up trust, love, and an open heart, even though the process included complaining, tears, laughter, and surrendering to my childlike wonder. They have enhanced every single part of my life. I look forward to what the future holds for me as they continue to share their wisdom and unconditional love.

Linda Berger

WAKING FROM THE TIDAL WAVE

A tidal wave of sorrow and tears startled me awake as it washed through my heart. Grasping for help, I called on the highest of Divine light and love. My Akashic Record Keepers gave me something to hold onto amidst the heart-wrenching flashbacks.

Waves of radiant, loving Akashic energies met the ferocity of stormy grief, enfolding me with calm.

I had entered the eye of the storm, where the winds and rain ebbed. My sobbing eased, and a clearing opened. I felt uplifted and lighter. But an anchor of painful emotions continued to clang around.

The velocity of this grief, decades after coming to terms with the loss of my dear friend, took me by surprise. For twenty-one years, this sudden loss had been finding ways to the surface. Now it demanded to be recognized, understood, and healed.

I asked my Akashic Record Keepers to travel back in time so I could release this pain once and for all. An immediate, expansive sensation swept into my heart, then opened my mind's eye. I could see into the vastness of the sky, which then expanded into an ocean-like sense of consciousness. I felt both sky and sea together, calm and peaceful, extending infinitely in all directions. My grief was absorbed into the beginning of time and simply changed form.

When I asked for help to clear the root of the pain that had flooded my psyche that morning, I saw yet another opening. This one led me into the vastness of an inky, indigo mystery. I could view the void of creation itself.

Observing this mystery of creation, a sense of safety enveloped me. My body responded with a deep sigh of relief. The ease, expansive quiet, peace, and weightlessness I felt were a distinct contrast to the dense sorrow and flashbacks I'd experienced. The grief was now a distant memory.

But... where are all the souls in this mystery? I wondered. *Where is the sense of connection?*

The Akashic Record Keepers showed me the vastness of space and stars that went far beyond individual humans on Earth. This was their answer: the far-reaching, multidimensional connections. Another range of high-frequency energy waves enfolded me and the constrictions in my mind, heart, and body eased even further. I felt that something new was forming as my thoughts melted into this vastness.

Yes, yes, yes! I thought, welcoming something so different from the pain. This felt anciently familiar, yet also foreign. I could sense that grief was no longer anchored in my heart. My heart, mind, and body embraced this welcoming *yes* to life and love.

As my grief continued to shift into the expansive, soothing mysteries of creation, I felt new appreciation for my friend. I wrote her a love letter with the caring energies that were filling my heart.

As I began to write, I realized that this morning was the twenty-first anniversary of her death.

For you, my friend Barbara... twenty-one years ago today:

When we first exchanged a healing, I didn't know my visions of dolphins held a prophesy of life-changing proportions. I didn't know we'd be sharing an adventure that directed our lives, or that I'd be present at your death after ten years of friendship.

Our innocent trip to swim with the dolphins, which we'd dreamed of for years, was supposed to mark my resignation from teaching. Instead, the transition was significantly larger than my career shift or your move to another state. We were embarking on a journey that was bigger than either of us could have imagined.

And yet, our souls knew something we did not yet understand. We had planned the trip of a lifetime—not knowing it was perfectly timed for your departure. This would be your send-off, as the dolphins circled near our boat in Key West.

We learned later from Captain Victoria that she'd never seen the dolphins circle her boat before. Two decades later, I learned that the energy of dolphins has been connected to special beings who are about to transition out of their bodies. Your arrangement to call in the dolphins to honor and send you off, my friend, was so fitting. They appeared to call you back to the stars, the mystery of life without your body.

The depth and scope of orchestration continued to unfold. Pegasus, the helicopter, flew you to Miami, where you could be surrounded by angels in human bodies. It took eleven teachers of healing, beloved partners, and a compassionate hospital staff to hold space to help you "drop your wrapper." My gratitude for their angel-human presence is immeasurable.

I spent years of wading through grief, anger, and despair before I understood that experiencing this with you was an honor.

My friend, thank you for showing the way, for being a lighthouse and a beacon for our hearts. Thank you for asking us to see ourselves as treasures.

My friend, I accept the treasures of me and of you, in all your forms.

Part Two

With all my love, Sandy

And so, grief awoke me and melted into love.

Sandy Rakowitz

MESSAGES OF LOVE

I'd spent an action-packed thirty-six hours with my beloved nieces, playing board games, laughing amongst squeals about cute boys on the TV screen, and enjoying stories of school life and teenage crushes. Exhausted but happy, I had dropped them off with their mother and returned home to enjoy a quiet evening. I didn't know that tragedy was about to strike.

When the phone rang. I was tempted to ignore it, but my brother's second wife rarely called me.

"He's gone," she wailed.

"What?"

"He fell and hit his head."

My brother, my only sibling, had had some close-call visits to the ICU in the past year because of alcoholism, which he had hidden for years. But I still was unprepared for this. His new business as a repair person seemed to be taking off. He finally had agreed to start an outpatient rehab program on Monday. I'd thought he was turning a corner.

"He died in the ambulance before he got to the hospital," my sister-in-law sobbed.

Part Two

Images of our shared history overwhelmed me: holding my brother as a newborn when I was three, playing with our dogs in the front yard. The year we marveled that "Santa came early" to bring us bikes. I remembered the day we found a perfect hawk feather nestled in a tree after I told him my power animal was a hawk. We'd even shared an apartment in Boulder when we were in our twenties.

Now I would have to call his daughters and share this tragic news.

Oh John, how could you leave your girls? I wondered. *How could that little boy I grew up with die in his forties?*

The family safety net that I was born into felt flimsy now. Who else would share these memories with me? Who could I ask the silly questions that popped into my mind, like where did our dog Tessa sleep when we were kids? Mom had dementia and Dad had never noticed those types of details.

I ached for my brother's daughters and everyone who had loved him. At the hospital, in shock as we stood with his body, I struggled to stay focused. Mom was using tissues to wipe away the fluids coming out of his mouth, still trying to care for her son, even now. She would then try to use the same tissue to blot her tears, if I didn't exchange it with a fresh one. We still didn't know if Covid had played a role in his death, so we had to stay safe, despite our grief.

He had complained of having the flu over Christmas, so I hadn't visited him. I suspected drinking was the major culprit, but there might have been other factors. We'd never know. The hospital didn't test him for Covid as part of the autopsy.

"My Johnny," Mom kept sobbing. She wore a lost expression now, more than her middle stage of dementia usually created. She would be even less connected to this world with her beloved son gone.

The months flew by, blurred by tears as I spent time caring for Mom so my father could leave the house; my mother, my best friend and soul sister, could not be left alone anymore. For fifteen months, she paced all day, lost, unreachable with words as her dementia progressed. She refused to eat or drink as the hospice aides administered morphine. Yet her body persisted.

At this final stage of dementia, I could no longer feel her presence in her body. She was starving and shutting down.

As an occupational therapist who had worked with dementia patients, I knew the disease would continue to slowly destroy her. She progressively lost her memory and then the use of her legs, her voice, and her comprehension to follow the simplest of directions. Then she lost her trunk muscles, her ability to smile, her arms and hands, and then the ability to swallow. At the end, she could not even close her eyes… and now her autonomic nervous system was desperately clinging to life, forcing her to breathe with labored, rattling gasps that shook her whole withered body.

It was horrific to watch. I hated this brutal ending for her, but there was nothing I could do to change the timeline of her death. I talked to her, held her hand, and said prayers with her. I sobbed and begged her spirit to please go and be at peace. She finally passed during the night. She was only seventy-three.

While I believed in a rich and peaceful afterlife as well as reincarnation, I wasn't prepared for the raw emotion that came with the loss of people so dear to me. I felt untethered as parts of me reached out to feel the presence of John and Mom.

I kept wondering, *Could I still connect with them? Should I? Where was their essence? What were they doing now?*

I began a course of study with the Akashic Records. It was perfect timing. Connecting with my record keepers helped me cope and brought welcome peace—even if just for moments—while I was grieving. My Akashic Record Keepers showed me how to ask to connect to their higher selves, though it was not a guarantee they would communicate with me. I did receive messages from my mother during these "talks." She said she would visit me through birds, which she had loved.

Part Two

Just a few hours after her passing, a bird sweetly sang atop the backyard wall. On and on she joyfully and proudly warbled, lifting my heart.

"Hi Mom," I said, smiling through my tears.

A couple of months later, my father decided he wanted to move closer to me. Just after a realtor showed us a house three blocks away from mine, a bright orange bird in the bushes caught my eye.

"What is that?" I asked my husband.

"I think it is a scarlet tanager," he said. "I've only seen one once before in my thirty-five years of living in Northern Colorado!"

I felt this special sighting was Mom telling me she liked the house and that she was somehow helping. She must have been. Although four different parties bid on that house, my Dad's bid won.

A few days later, I heard my Mom's voice in my head saying, *For God's sake Erika, change your sheets!* I laughed and felt even more resolutely that she was nearby, mothering me. As I sorted through her belongings and helped pack up their house for the move, I cried often, but recalling her comment often made me smile.

The thing that was saddest about my mother and brother passing was that so much of their lives seemed unfinished. Mom had always wanted to write books about the spirit of water, the evolution of personal growth through her family line, and the unique counseling process that she developed. I gathered her notes and the books she was using as references, thinking maybe she could channel them through me. I opened my Akashic Records to ask about it, and the record keepers said, *We'll just let your Mom speak.*

Mother's voice, loud and clear said, *Don't you dare try to finish my unfinished business honey. It's not your job, my dear, it's mine. I can still work on those things in other ways, in other lives. If you feel moved to write something with me, then we'll talk about it, but you have your own life to attend to. You focus on what you came here to do. Don't feel responsible for my unfinished work. Don't take that on, pumpkin. Okay?*

Her voice was urgent, loving but firm. Her message helped me to understand something on a deeper level: our souls keep growing and working through issues to continue expanding and healing. We make new soul plans to accomplish new things. Though this made sense on an intellectual level, my heart was struggling with that idea when it came to my own loved ones. Yet Mom had told me even her unfinished business was part of her journey.

As the grief of losing my mom began to loosen its grip, I thought more about my brother. Though tears didn't come as often now, I still wondered what his soul was up to. Where was he? Why didn't I feel his spirit?

Then I had a poignant dream about him. Side-by-side, we top-roped down a thirty-foot wall, and with twenty feet remaining, he jumped from the wall, landing in a perfect superhero lunge. He was ripped and vibrant. He walked in this video-game-like world as if he owned the place, and then the game began. Hundreds of people drew hidden weapons of all kinds, keen on pursuit–of him!

All of them had a bounty to kill him and wanted to be the one to collect the fee. Could he survive such a fate? It seemed impossible. Yet he had a confident smile as he dodged, fought, and ran. I awoke with an uneasy feeling. Maybe his soul was not at peace at all—or worse, maybe he was in danger!

The next day, a perfect hawk feather appeared in my front yard. It was like the one we had found together thirty-six years before. I hadn't seen one since that day, so I took note and felt it surely was John contacting me.

Opening my Akashic Records later that day, I tried the technique my record keepers showed me—and my brother came to talk to me! I was relieved to hear him explain that he has been allowed to visit me from time to time, to help me out of tough situations.

A few months after he died, I had been driving at sixty m.p.h. when a deer stepped into my path about five feet away. I tried to slam on the brakes, but hit the gas instead. My Prius swerved and actually went up on its two right-side wheels before landing perfectly, far past the deer. Somehow the

Part Two

deer, myself, and the car were unscathed. I had felt that my brother had jumped into my body and did that stunt driving for me, because that was his driving style—not mine!

Now he apologized and told me how much he missed and loved my Dad and me. *I'm working through some stuff. It's like a video game in some ways, what I am doing. I get to practice here, and I want and need a lot of practice before I come back into a body. I want to do better next time. I have asked to come back to be with my daughters. Even if I must be a freaking goldfish or a fly on a wall, I want to be in physical form near them. I do get to visit them with angels, but it's not the same. I'd love to come back as a puppy, because then I could snuggle and play with them, but I'm not ready for that yet. I'm still mad at their stepdad and would be tempted to bite him, but I'm not allowed to do that. So I will keep practicing being in a body again in a simulation-like a video game, until I've learned enough to be and act differently. I want you and the girls to be proud of me. I don't feel pain here, except when I do the video game and practice being in a body again. I don't think about drinking here. I can leave the game anytime and feel completely loved and supported. I'm good. You don't need to worry about me.*

Since getting his message, I have stopped worrying. A wonderful friend said to me, "You'll get to the point that, when you think of the ones you lost, you will smile instead of cry."

As I write this, a hawk is calling out, perched in a nearby pine tree. It makes me smile.

Erika Osmann Mason

A CHANGE IN MY LIFE

I was perched on the edge of my hotel room chair, trembling with anticipation, worried that my first solo session wouldn't work.

Frustrated, I cried out, "Masters, teachers, and loved ones, I am going to sit here until I hear something from you!"

This journey had started when a friend told me about a woman who had given him an amazing reading. She sounded great, however, I set the information aside for a future time.

That time came one day while I was cleaning my desk. The woman's number seemed to pop right out of the drawer! I was led to pick up the phone immediately and call her. A week later, I was on the phone again, getting ready for my reading.

In the first moments of that call, she explained something to me, about me, that I had never told anyone. Not even my husband, with whom I shared almost everything, knew this. I was left speechless as she described another lifetime, in Paris, when that husband had left our child and me. I never knew why he left. It created a sadness that had come back to me in this lifetime, and perhaps to other lifetimes as well. *How could she have known about that sadness?* Most importantly, while hearing about this, the sadness left me.

Part Two

She then told me that I had done readings for others in a past life but did not have the right tools in that incarnation. She implied that life had not ended well.

What.... What is she saying? I asked myself. I had often thought that I might have been burned at the stake in another life because of things I knew that others did not. I had never taken this too seriously. Yet here she was confirming my thoughts and using the very word that meant so much to me in this life: tools.

Growing up, I was taught that, if you are going to do any job well, you must have the proper tools. As soon as she made the statement about tools, I desperately wanted them. In fact, I knew that I had to have them!

And that was how I found myself leaving Florida to drive to Asheville, NC, that fateful afternoon. I didn't know that my quest for the proper tools and the next two days were about to change my life.

As soon as I pulled off the highway, I saw a sign on the side of an old, rickety building that advertised a product my husband and I had been involved with years before. That business had ended abruptly; I still longed for it and the life we'd had then, even twenty-two years later.

"Oh boy, Levine," I muttered to myself. "This is a sign of things to come. What are the odds of you seeing this sign, now? You're in for something here. Are you sure you want to do this?"

I didn't know what this sign had to do with my being here for this class; however, I was intrigued and compelled to go forward.

As I sat waiting for our class to begin, I was thinking about what we were going to learn. I remembered being told that I had done readings for others. *Hmm... but how? How did it happen? What would it feel like?*

All the questions I hadn't asked myself came flooding into my mind now, along with a bit of fear as I wondered if I would be able to do a reading in the proper way.

Everyone chatted and talked excitedly as they caught up with friends or introduced themselves to new people. I looked around the room at the beautifully worn wooden floors and the table at the front of the room where precious stones—amethyst, lapis, quartzite, and red jasper—had been scattered. Two chairs were vacant. I assumed one was for the teacher. The tension from everyone's excitement to get this day started was apparent.

At nine a.m., a dark-haired woman entered the room. She said she was our teacher and introduced a friend she had brought with her. The friend, who had the most beautiful blue, compassionate eyes, reminded me of many of my father's people. When I exchanged smiles with her, I knew that everything was going to be okay.

The teacher asked us to introduce ourselves and gave us an overview of the two days. She then held up a picture and said, "Look at this picture, then use your journals to write what you see in it. There are no right or wrong answers."

She said that we would come back to the picture later. I couldn't guess why we had done this exercise, but it felt like one more piece of a puzzle that was being assembled.

As we turned the pages of our materials, we learned more about the Akashic Records. There was a specific sacred procedure for opening them, and doing so required trust. Hearing these words gave me great comfort.

We practiced opening and closing our Akashic Records and doing different exercises. *I'm getting physically tired doing this practice work*, I thought.

Next, she asked us to open our records so we could ask the masters, teachers, and loved ones to tell us more about the picture she'd shown. I was curious as I carefully opened my records. I reread what I had written earlier and asked the question. Immediately, I started to receive information. It was so different from what I had written when I'd seen the picture before. I became a little more confident.

Part Two

Who am I kidding? I'm thrilled to be receiving information! Up to that point in the day, I was not sure I was really in touch with the Akasha. Cautiously, I thought, *I can do this.* I couldn't explain exactly how I had received the information. It was as though, somehow, it had been implanted within me.

We were given homework and told to be back at one p.m. the next day. I was a bit spacey as I left the center, so I stamped my feet on the ground, as we had been told to do. Our teacher had explained that the spaciness, which felt like being light-headed, came from the amount of energy we had used that day.

"Ground yourselves before you drive," she had cautioned.

Our homework question felt huge. I was to open my records and ask about my life mission. I tried that evening, but it proved fruitless, so I closed my records again. I felt I might be too tired. Maybe it would work in the morning.

Awaking early, I sat at the little round table in my room with my notebook, my prayer cards, and a pen.

"I am ready," I declared.

I took a deep breath. I opened my Akashic Records and asked the question. "What is my mission in this life?"

For a while, I didn't hear or feel anything. I wasn't being implanted with any information.

I asked in another way. "Can you tell me what I am supposed to do in this life?"

Still nothing. I sat there for a good forty-five minutes but received nothing, no matter how I asked the question.

That was when I made my desperate plea and threatened to stay in my chair until answers came. Finally, amazingly, information began pouring into my being. I could hardly scribble fast enough to keep up with everything I was receiving.

The Akashic Record Keepers must have felt the need to help me get closure on the mystery of why I had seen the sign on the old, rickety building.

The sign was an opportunity for us to give you a lesson about learning to really trust again, they said. *You must trust if you are to go forward in life.*

They continued, *It is also about picking up the pieces and moving on, even in the face of great loss. Through loss, we can find great strength. In that strength, we can learn to trust. In that trusting, we find help and gratitude and more love.*

I had goosebumps of excitement, knowing that I had connected and received from the masters, teachers, and loved ones during what I considered my first solo session in the Akashic Records. My heart was so full of love and thankfulness. It was almost more than I could comprehend and felt overwhelmingly beautiful. In those moments, and many since then, I knew I had been Divinely, gently, touched. I had never experienced anything like this in my life until then.

When I walked back into the class at one that afternoon, our teacher looked at me and asked, "What happened to you? You look refreshed and renewed."

I'm normally quiet, but I couldn't wait to tell everyone what had happened that morning. Since then, the Akashic Records have had a most profound influence on my life. Journaling to access this information gives me a different way to deal with my thoughts and receive Divine answers to my questions.

Those two days of classes changed my life and the lives of those around me—and there is still so very much to learn.

Stephany Levine

SOULS INTERWINED

The universe was orchestrating a meeting. First Maya, one of my closest friends, called to ask if she could visit on Easter weekend. I had last seen her the year before, when we and our mutual friend Alice took a powerful and transformative trip to Sedona. At that time, she and I had not seen each other for thirty years and we were both in the midst of traumatic divorces. The trip was the beginning of a profound, three-way friendship and clear alignment of our individual spiritual journeys.

I was thrilled to hear from Maya, but a bit puzzled. Her divorce had left her in a difficult financial position, and a plane ticket for a short weekend was expensive. In the coming days, I was even more surprised to receive a call from Alice, who asked if she could fly in from California on the same weekend! Alice rarely traveled—certainly not all the way to the Twin Cities for a brief weekend visit. Hmm. My antennae was beginning to go up. *What was going on?*

In the days before Easter, I received yet another call from my brother, who lived several hours away with his family. He shared that they would be driving down to my town to visit his in-laws for Easter. Could they borrow my kids for the entire weekend?

Part Two

Now I was sure some plan was being hatched in the nonphysical realms. I gave my brother a resounding "Yes!" without a second thought. To my knowledge, my brother had no idea about my friends coming in, and he'd never asked to take the kids before. A familiar energy was building and I could feel purposeful events were about to unfold.

Easter weekend arrived and my friends flew in as scheduled. Alice's birthday happened to fall on that weekend. One of the first evenings of the visit, I offered her a qigong healing session as a gift. I had been doing energy healing since 2007 and had experienced a leap in development since I began training with a local qigong master a few months earlier. Alice eagerly accepted. She sat on a chair in the middle of the family room and I went about my healing process.

As I neared the end of the session, I became aware of one or more nonphysical beings present. When I mentioned this was happening, I felt familiar tingles all over my body and became more strongly aware of one particular energy. We soon identified our visitor and with the aid of Alice's clairvoyant sensitivities, began to communicate. I found I was able to sense the essence of messages, and we would then inquire for more details.

It soon became clear that a line of spirits had formed, wanting their turn to be identified. Alice was touched and appreciated quite a few visits from family and friends, both living and deceased. We were all delighted with the experience.

The following evening, Alice suggested I offer Maya a turn to receive healing, so that she might feel included. To my amazement, as I began working on Maya, I again felt the clear presence of nonphysical beings. We began to have an experience nearly identical to the evening before. One spirit after another stepped forward and offered a message or merely wanted their presence acknowledged. Both friends happily assisted me with interpreting the communication from each visitor.

Maya and Alice chatted in delight as I rested quietly on the couch for a few minutes. Suddenly, I slipped into what I can only describe as a semi-trance-like state. I felt fully aware, yet with a sense that I was in the back seat of a car where a master energy had taken the wheel and the microphone–or in this case, my voice. I was not frightened, as I sensed that I could step forward any time I chose. I felt eager to hear what this higher energy perspective had to share.

Initially, I saw and felt emotions from a past life near Nepal around 1790. I was female and the souls of Alice and Maya were also both present in female form. As I connected more deeply, I was overcome by grief and the deep emotional pain of a traumatic experience unfolding before me. I cried out to Alice and Maya (in the present time): "You hurt me!"

The energy I perceived spoke a few words, but I felt myself resist describing everything I was seeing, afraid to interrupt the vision by continuing to speak aloud.

I heard my friends say, "We are so sorry."

They had quickly understood that I was seeing a past life and began gently asking questions. I was crying so hard, I could not speak, but it was easy for me to confirm yes and no without interrupting the experience. They mirrored back what I saying, and I guided them to an accurate understanding of the scene. I could see that my then-husband had gone on a long hunting trip with men from our village. The hunting party had returned without him. I felt my fear of a tragedy turn to humiliation when the returned hunters told me of stopping in another village on their way home.

They had encountered an aging couple with an attractive, young daughter living in the village. This family was clearly desperate. They had no male support and needed someone to make repairs and physical preparations for their survival. The family quickly spotted a good catch for the unwed daughter and the rescuer they needed: my husband. He sent the rest of the

Part Two

party home with the proceeds of their hunt and stayed to help the woman and her parents. He enjoyed the adventure, attentions, and flattery for a while. After a significant absence, he disclosed that he had a family of his own and headed home.

I saw clearly that my husband in that life was none other than the husband I had recently divorced in present time, and that his energy was much the same: highly skilled and protective, but equally prone to trade responsibility for pleasure and entertainment. I saw that the young woman was the same soul as my friend Alice, and that Maya was present as well, as my sister in my home village. The culture did not appear to be a kind one. As my sister witnessed the hurtful rumors and humiliation when my husband had not returned, she hissed at me cruelly that it was because I was so ugly.

I was aware from my vantage point that, in this tribe, female beauty was power. A woman's rank and even survival could depend on it. Our nomadic, tribal culture also valued survival skills and physical capability, and the villagers ascribed a hierarchy to the eligible men. I saw my sister's jealousy and resentment that I had been chosen by the prized bachelor in our village, a man who had both looks and provider skills, while she remained unwed and with an unknown future. Life felt unfair, and this was her chance for a little justice.

From a bird's-eye view, I felt compassion for all three of us as we played our various roles in this drama. I felt pity for my husband of both lifetimes, who seemed childlike and without a spiritual path. I also realized that a spiritually wise village elder from whom I received guidance was the soul of my son in this life, Jacob. I felt immense gratitude for his compassion and higher perspective that supported me through that trauma.

After sharing the scene I was witnessing with my friends, my body suddenly doubled over in pain in present time and was racked with deep sobbing. I was crying so hard at one point that no sound came from my throat.

Suddenly, I felt and heard an energy release from my middle abdomen. It was as if a large pocket of air found an exit at my skin surface and came whooshing out, much like an inflated balloon would release its contents. I knew the painful experience of the past lifetime was being released and healed. The emotional pain left me, along with the energy that rapidly dispersed, leaving me feeling distinctly lighter.

After a rest, Alice asked if we might hear of other lifetimes she suspected we must have had together, since the three of us obviously had a strong soul connection. I recall sharing that we had all been priestesses together in one lifetime. In another life, around 1400, we were killed for being witches. We had also been physicians and healers in many incarnations.

I described that one of the physician lifetimes had been traumatic for all of us as we cared for the wounded in a war. Images of men with fighting with spears and shields began to appear, and I referenced Alexandria and a Trojan horse. I explained that our legends of Troy are based on real events and that we had witnessed many horrors.

After learning about many fascinating lifetimes in our collective Akashic Records, Alice asked if I had ever been killed for my abilities. I immediately saw myself as a young boy who was a family friend of King Solomon. The king unexpectedly appointed me to some coveted position of power, because he trusted my healing gifts. Someone expecting the role murdered me in a fit of jealousy. I saw that the king was fond of me and was sad and guilt-ridden for this treachery. I then came out of the trance.

My friends were amazed and exclaimed how cool it was to be a part of this. I was both fascinated and drained by the experience, but briefly back in present awareness. I got up for some refreshment and returned to relax while the other women chatted. I soon felt myself slip back in semi-trance, and another energy I trusted came forward to speak. The energy was a higher vibration from the Akasha and had access to knowledge of all our lifetimes.

Part Two

I heard myself say "If you would like, I will share a lifetime for each of you that is the origin of a pattern that is no longer serving you. Get paper and take notes."

Maya had lived a life in an Inuit community as a male and had lost two children in separate tragedies, years apart. She had experienced unfair blame and lowered stature in her community, and complete marital rejection following the loss of her wife's favorite child, along with deep shame and unwarranted guilt in addition to her own grief. These traumas have continued to affect her empowerment and ability to love herself in subsequent lives.

Alice experienced a particularly horrific lifetime as a healer when she witnessed her entire community die of a water-borne illness, one by one, and could do nothing to save them. The pain of the suffering she witnessed in all those in her community, including the children, and feelings of failure in her efforts to prevent any deaths continue to impact her beliefs around health and her ability for self-love.

I had lived a lifetime in the 900s in an area that is now Turkey in which I had been married to the same ex-husband as in Nepal and my current lifetime. My family included every member of my current family of origin. I saw that after I experienced an enlightenment of sorts, I refused to observe the community practices and beliefs. My husband falsely accused me of failing to perform my marital duties. To "fix" me, the villagers tried various tortures before deciding on a punishment of public stoning. I saw the faces of my family as they crowded towards me, shouting in contempt, and felt horror and the shock of betrayal as I uttered "Group mind." I recognized the energetic parallels to this lifetime of unhealed emotional abuse, particularly from childhood. I believe that I likely chose all of my current family members to seek healing for that lifetime and the emotional patterns it birthed.

I was grateful that, through the experience of accessing my Akashic Records, I was able to help my friends and myself begin to understand and heal our false beliefs and identities that bring our greatest suffering and limitation.

Marcia Lowry

HEALER ON A HEALING PATH

Seven years ago, I had a freak accident that yanked the rug from under my feet and altered the course of my life. I was unable to work; loss of mobility, chronic pain, and post-traumatic stress confined me to my home. Even taking care of my basic needs became a challenge. I needed assistance to take a bath. This was devastating. I went from independent and self-reliant to requiring help from others.

Everything that I loved to do—my hobbies, my social life, going out to visit friends, doing yoga—were no longer possible. I fell apart and sank into despair.

My daily life consisted of excruciating, burning pain that kept me from sleeping. I took medications to keep the pain to a bearable level. I would eat, sit for five minutes, and then move back to my bed to recover from the effort, sweating profusely. I felt betrayed, desperate, and alone, but also angry. I refused to be condemned to living this way.

At last, I found the courage to start my healing journey. I tried every medical department, going from doctor to doctor and spending too much of our limited resources, hoping to get better. Herbal and alternative medicine didn't help. Nothing made much difference to the pain.

Part Two

I registered for workshops, classes, and angel circles, always hoping to find a cure. Akashic Records ads would randomly cross my path, but I always ignored them.

One day, I told the angels, "Either help me or put me out of my misery! I can't take this level of pain anymore."

The next time I saw an Akashic Records ad, all my senses were awake again. I explained to my husband that this was no coincidence, but a message, a sign. Every little particle in me had put this opportunity in front of me. I suddenly felt hopeful. This might be a way to improve my quality of life.

We booked a healing consultation. During the consultation, I felt an energy shift, as if a weight was lifted off my shoulders, reducing my pain to a bearable level for the first time. This restored my faith. It felt just short of a miracle. *What else could it do?*

At that moment, I knew that learning the Akashic Records was part of my Divine path. *This could help so many people*, I thought. I became a student.

Early in the course, I could only sit for five minutes in class; then I'd have to lie down to listen to the rest of the course and then sleep for hours to recover from listening. I prayed, meditated, and did everything I was instructed to do. Today, I can sit for extended periods of time, enjoy a visit, and share a meal with my family.

I choose to be grateful. It has been a long road, but I move forward on my journey, one step at the time. The Akashic Records are always there, helping me stay grounded and present as I keep trying to get better. Now that I have them in my life, my fear and despair have vanished, replaced by faith in the possibilities of what can be.

Caroline Lambert

I FOUND MY MAYAN TEMPLE

The speaker's presentation about the Akashic Records was mesmerizing. I knew I had to get a reading from her while I was still at the metaphysical conference.

When I asked her a question, she said, "Wait! I need to tell you something important first. Did you know you were a Mayan high priestess not too long ago?"

"No," I said, startled. What's 'not too long ago'?"

"A thousand years ago. Do you know about the Mayans?"

"I know a little bit."

"You have some work to do with the Mayans in this lifetime."

Fascinated by what she had said, I began researching the Mayan culture the moment I got home, but little information was available at that time. I became very curious about being a Mayan priestess. I'd always been attracted to Belize. Now I felt a calling to go there. I wanted to see if I recognized anything.

In 1998, I met a couple who told me about a shaman who was taking a group down to the Mayan lands on the Spring Equinox. This is the time when the sun hits the Kukulcan Pyramid at Chichen Itza in such a way that the shadow of a snake appears to crawl down the structure's side. The journey would include other Mayan temples. I was excited to hear of this opportunity and arranged to make the trip.

One of the many temples we visited was Uxmal, which had been a school where healing, astronomy, mathematics, shamanism, priest and high priestess preparation, and initiations had been taught. The ancient building had been used as a mystery school and ceremonial center for thousands of years.

Our shaman guide said this was where the priestesses were trained. My reader had told me that I'd spent my younger years completing the thirty-three steps of knowledge to priestess, and that most people did not complete all the steps. *Was this where I had studied?*

During the hours we were there, I walked the whole property. I climbed the Pyramid of the Magician, but still did not feel anything. I got to the top of another pyramid—called the Grand Pyramid—which has macaw birds carved on the top of it. It felt peaceful there, but I didn't recognize anything. Disappointment began to overtake my enthusiasm.

That night, we stayed at a nearby hotel. At sunset, as I gazed out from my hotel balcony, I received a stunning vision. I saw myself standing on the Grand Pyramid. I wore a white dress with long, flowing sleeves. My hair was black, cut short over my eyes, and I wore a headband. A male shaman was initiating me.

The shaman was handsome with long, dark hair and wore garments of turquoise and red. In Native American culture, those colors mean earth and sky. As he performed the initiation, hundreds of cheering people filled the courtyard in front of the pyramid.

The vision was so clear. Uxmal, in the Yucatan, was the place I had received my teachings and training. *But where was I from and where did I live after my training?*

Several years passed before I had these answers. Another Akashic Records reader told me I had been born in Belize.

"The people in Belize needed a high priestess, and you were chosen at the age of five to train at a school to fill this role. You remained there until you were twenty-five," the Akasha reader shared.

She continued, "When you had completed all the steps needed to become a high priestess, you returned to Belize. You served as that community's high priestess until you were quite old, in your late nineties. Your name was Amara."

Now I knew why I'd always felt a longing for Belize. It had been home.

As I watched documentaries of the temples in Belize, I kept being drawn to a place called Xunantunich. I found many photos of the temple, but not much about its history.

In 2019, I made another trip to Belize to visit Xunantunich. This time, I hired a Mayan guide who had lived in that area all his life. I told him I was a sound healer and musician, and my name is ThunderBeat. That's all I told him.

We walked together up to the large, main temple as I tuned in to its energy, trying to determine if I recognized anything. Three huge glyphs with many symbols adorned the temple walls. I asked my guide what they meant.

"The one on the left means sound, and the one on the right means music," he said.

Excitedly, I told him again that I am a sound healer and a musician. I asked, "What does the glyph mean in the middle?"

"Thunder Chac," he replied. "The Rain God."

I almost fell over. "I think this was my temple in a past life. This is why I came here."

"Yes, this was a female temple. We call her the Queen of the Sky," he said.

"High priestess from the stars," I mused.

He gave me a strange look.

Part Two

"My name in that lifetime was Amara."

The guide's mouth dropped open. He looked deeply into my eyes and said, "Your name is embedded on the side of this pyramid."

We walked down and he pointed it out. I meditated there for a while and heard a message saying people came from miles away to celebrate and receive healings here. In a vision, I saw many Mayan people dancing and celebrating in the courtyard of the pyramid.

I was home.

Devara ThunderBeat

HEALING HARMFUL TAPES

For twenty-five years, I balanced a stressful career with the awareness that something even greater was waiting for me. Yet when I first tried to read the Akashic Records, after taking a class, I saw nothing … absolute blackness! I finished the course but thought, *I guess this isn't for me!*

Four months later, my guides told me that I am meant to read for others. I asked a friend if I could perform a practice reading on her. As I said the access prayer, I had butterflies in my stomach, but then it happened: I immediately entered her Akashic Records and found myself looking down on different scenes from her life.

Everything I needed to know began to unfold before my eyes. I couldn't believe it! The Akashic Records were what I had been looking for my entire life. That day, I decided to start doing readings for others.

My readings take place in the quantum field. My guides provide what I call my "quantum screen," an image in my mind's eye upon which I watch messages that they give me. Scenes play out as if I were watching a movie in a large theater. When the time is right, my guides make suggestions that might help the client heal. Such healings often transform my clients. They also allow

Part Two

me to add more empathy and understanding to my life, because I can see people beyond their earthly experience.

During one reading, my client and I were focusing on a potential career choice. I was suspended in the field inside her Akashic Records. Our reading was done remotely, but she was on my quantum screen. As she discussed her choices, I began to hear a strange chattering in the background, as if dozens of people were talking softly at once. I searched the area, trying to find the source of the sounds. Behind my client, I noticed a huge, gnarled oak tree. Its branches were knotted around something, but I couldn't make out what it was.

As I drew nearer, I saw dozens of small TVs that included video tape players. The VCR element let me know I was dealing with events that dated back to her childhood. Each TV set was playing a different scene in her life where someone had scarred her with their words. Her deceased father, who had been critical and emotionally distant, was the voice on many of the TVs. His harmful words played continuously in the background of her mind, infinitely looping and drilling negativity deep into her soul.

I described what I saw to my client and told her that it is hard for her to move ahead in life because of these "tapes" reverberating in her soul. There must have been at least fifty TV sets spewing negativity as they sat in the twisted branches of the looming tree, holding her painful memories.

Her deceased father stepped into the scene. I decided to ask for his help. *How can we heal all these years of damage? Should we use a saw, or maybe an ax, to chop down the tree?*

Love, he responded. *We heal with love.*

I told my client her dad was with us and that together, with love, we were going to stop these tapes from playing. She and her dad walked up to the first TV. He took her right hand and gently placed it on top of the knot that had formed in the branch to hold the TV in place. He then put his right hand on top of hers and said, *I am sorry. Please forgive me.*

The TV stopped playing and fell to the ground.

They moved to the next one and he repeated his apology; that TV set also released and fell. They moved through five knots on the tree and then suddenly, all the remaining sets broke off the tree and clattered to the ground—and all the tapes went silent.

I knew that having freedom from the constant, negative mental chatter would allow her to move forward with her life, without being limited by damaging words from her past.

"It might take time to get used to the silence," I advised. Constant noise had been all she had ever known.

I asked the record keepers to infuse her with golden light until she could find peace with the adjustment.

I told her that, at any time in the future, if she heard residual noise from these tapes, she was to look over her left shoulder and see that the tree is gone.

"The noise has stopped, and the words cannot haunt you any longer," I said. "The energy has been transformed!"

Through the beautiful Akashic Records, she had been set free.

Renee Teresa

RELEASED FROM ROPES

I was surprised when an image of myself appeared in my head. Clear as day, I was in a darkened corner, tied in ropes, and feeling incredibly sad and dejected. *You need to get to the Akashic Records and investigate,* was the message I received.

I have been trained to do work in the Akashic Records for others for the last fifteen years, but it took a while to truly feel comfortable doing readings and clearings for myself, too.

I went to my office and healing space and took out my favorite crystals. Taking longer than usual to truly honor the process, I entered my Akashic Records.

My first stop was the area outside the doorway I imagine before I enter. I felt a lot of beautiful beings there—angels, guides, masters, and teachers—and they were all there addressing me. They asked if I knew how much my work in the records had helped others. *Why have you not given yourself credit for the work you've done?*

Sitting next to my file cabinet, which contains more than 800 records of readings I've done, I felt guided to put my hand on the cabinet. An energy filled with love surged through me. It was as if the hundreds of people I'd

Part Two

done readings for, and the ripple effect from that, were thanking me. I was also finally able to sink into gratitude not just for this work but for the time and energy I had put into learning and showing others how to access their Akashic Records. Tears were streaming down my face, tears of gratitude and deep love for the work I have done and continue to do.

I then got the message, *You needed to receive this love before we show you the image you saw today.*

I was supported on both sides by guides as the door opened and we entered the Hall of Akashic Records. I picture it as a gigantic architectural triumph. The ceilings are so high you cannot see the top. The columns and desks are ornate, yet somehow comforting. The beings I see and feel there always emit love. Now, that love was magnified because I was still holding gratitude from the previous moments.

I was instructed to truly sink into love and gratitude as they revealed the vision again. I was a younger version of myself—whether this lifetime, another, or probably a combination. I was bound in a chair and looking so very sad.

My guides then handed me a huge pair of scissors and told me, *It is time to set that girl free.* I knew I did not need to be restrained anymore. As I started to cut the ropes, I felt deep compassion for this restrained little girl. I wept as I cut the ropes and told her, "It will be okay. It is time to be free."

When she was fully released, I hugged her and felt such love and relief from her in return.

Then the girl and the chair began to grow. The chair looked more like an ancient throne of some sorts. She was asked to take her place upon it—and now she and I were almost as one. I was told, *You have done the work. Now it is time to receive.*

The people I had helped—and some I did not recognize—honored me with gifts and hugs. I felt so much love for the work, for the magic of the records, and for my journey the last fifteen years. Yet I was hesitant to mount the throne. I heard, *Because of that humbleness, you are worthy of it.* I realized that we all deserve to feel like we are on a throne: worthy, loved, and respected. The moment was awash in tears.

I sat still for a bit and received, feeling the release. When I stood up, I felt strangely confident. I made my way back to the door, supported once more by my loving guides as I said goodbye. I paused outside to thank the other beings of light for their assistance.

When I returned, I was a bit weary from the crying, but also filled with so much love and light. Within me was a deeper sense of hope than I have had in a long while.

Jenny Mannion

TUNING IN TO THE AKASHA

The Akasha had always been a mysterious, mystical term to me. I wondered about it, but it seemed too abstract to ever get a grasp on, like the concepts of infinity or eternity. I assumed it would always be an elusive and incomprehensible idea that was way beyond me.

That changed one day as I walked through the forest in the early morning of a lovely, sunny day, enjoying the joyful singing of birds. Suddenly, walking toward me on the dirt path, was a friend I had not seen in ten years. She smiled and we talked briefly, promising to meet again.

A few days later, walking together beside a creek in a lush forest, she told me she had been helping clients by doing Akashic clearing sessions. My heart fluttered and my curiosity about this subject returned.

We watched dogs run on their leashes next to their caretakers and squirrels scampering in the trees. Under a spectacularly radiant sky with fluffy clouds drifting in carefree reverie, I told her that I was doing monthly reflexology sessions at a nearby psychic fair. She talked about her travels and her family.

I realized how much I had missed her kind presence at the temple, where we had met. After I got home, I meditated and thanked Source for bringing

Part Two

her back into my life. Her vibration was calming and healing. Soothing balm seemed to pour over and through me when I was in her stable, centered presence. There was none of the agitation I felt when I was with chatterbox people who were not good listeners.

My old friend traveled the world with a confident presence. I was so different. Because of PTSD, I usually felt like a bundle of scattered, confused thoughts and frayed nerves. I wanted what she had—to be unafraid of the world. Breathing into my heart, I felt it expand. I needed to be in her vibration again.

Later that day, I called to schedule an appointment with her for an Akashic clearing session. Explaining that I was dependent on a government disability check, I asked her if she would be willing to exchange treatments. I felt blessed when she said she would be glad to.

Her home was lovely and peaceful. Lavender and white orchids shone under tiny white raindrop lights that covered a large picture window. Spiritual sculptures and paintings, as well as crystals, glistened in the light. A serene vibration of the love and light of the Creator filled the air.

I needed more of this, I thought. When I went to parties filled with laughing, alcohol-drinking people, I felt unheard. I came home feeling empty. The powerful force of goodness in this home was calming me and nourishing my love-starved emotions.

She led me to a comfortable chair and instructed me to relax as she explained the Akashic clearing and how it worked. Skepticism clawed my heart.

Speaking in relaxing tones, she asked me to close my eyes and take myself to a past life that would give me some knowledge and understanding that I could apply to my current life. I felt as if I were moving through a tunnel, going deeper and deeper until I left the present time behind.

Suddenly, I saw myself. I was a beggar dressed in ragged old clothes, standing on a sidewalk. Well-dressed, wealthy people walked past me. I was awed by their confidence and suave sophistication. They seemed to have the world by its tail.

I needed to beg them for food, but I was afraid to ask for anything. I wanted to hide instead. Embarrassment overwhelmed me, and I felt adrift—like a completely helpless, hopeless non-entity.

I could feel the emotions of that incarnation. Life was passing me by. There was no way for me to take charge and become a wealth-earning, worthwhile citizen. I couldn't do anything but stand there, blank faced, in my stinking rags, too afraid to ask anyone for money. I watched successful people engage in their important activities and enjoy their lives with their friends and family while I suffered in invisible silence.

When my friend brought me back to the present, I had new compassion for myself. I had done my best, in this life, to live on my government disability check. I decided to stop comparing myself to others. Being different and isolated was not easy. However, there was always happiness to be found, if only I would look around.

I decided to work to improve my writing—and Source was right there, loving and healing me. Soon, I received an email saying that my story had been accepted to be published. I felt worthy, like those powerful people I had been mesmerized by lifetimes ago.

Sophia Moon

JUST A SATURDAY WORKSHOP

It was early one Saturday morning and my cousin and I were excited to attend a workshop at a local metaphysical store. The woman leading the class was a well-known healer who specialized in hypnosis and past-life regressions. These were somewhat new concepts to me, but I was eager to learn about my own past lives.

As a sensitive empath and energy worker, I always prepare myself and seal my energy with protection before entering a room filled with people I don't know. However, on this day we were rushed and had gotten lost on our way to the class, so it slipped my mind.

As we entered the store, I began to feel an overwhelming energy, which I assumed was coming from all the crystals in the store. It has always been hard for me to be in environments with such intense energy. I went straight to the restroom and splashed some water on my face and washed my hands, hoping to shift myself into a more grounded space.

As I walked to the room where everyone was gathered, I began to feel my body swaying a little. I was dizzy. I chose the closest seat to the door, in case I had to leave quickly. Then I closed my eyes and called in my guides, asking for support. Quickly, the feeling subsided.

Part Two

When the instructor introduced herself and the work we were about to do together, my body began to shiver and I felt chilled. These sensations sometimes served as a confirmation that my guides were with me. I was confident that I was in a good, protected space.

As we were being led into the hypnosis, I started to have flashes of different short stories. They were like tiny video clips shown in vivid, bright colors, as if I were watching teasers for movies. The instructor began to close the session and slowly brought us back into the room. She asked us to record our experiences during the regression with as much detail as we could recall. I began to write feverishly. I couldn't stop writing. I'd seen at least seven short stories in great detail.

As I wrote, I began to realize these movies were not about me. It felt like I was writing a fictional story, or even a fairy tale. The instructor approached and looked over my shoulder as she asked, "Are you a psychic medium?"

I had never been asked the question quite like that before. My cousin immediately laughed and confirmed, yes. I agreed.

The instructor returned to her chair and asked if I would share my experience. The many scenarios, I later found out, were the soul experiences of other people.

Each story that I read aloud was connected to someone in the circle. None of them were my own experiences. There were fifteen people in the circle, and half of them identified, even down to the smallest detail, with one of the stories I described.

As I spoke, the feelings of dizziness and nausea that I had walked into the session with started to dissolve. It became obvious that my guides had brought these experiences to me to confirm for each person. I had accessed the Akashic Records. This was a new gift.

Over time, after this experience, it became more obvious to me that not only was I able to access the Akashic Records, but I also began to see and feel timelines. It started with predictions of timelines around future events.

I developed the ability to ask and receive a physical feeling in my body to confirm days, months, and years. It felt like this psychic skill was an expanded version of my connection.

After practicing this for a while, it started to happen during readings with clients. I began to get these flashes of video clips "time-stamped" with years and centuries. Often, these portrayed incidents from ancient times. There usually were clues like clothing, animals, scenery, or modes of transportation that would confirm the exact time period.

I would begin by asking the person for permission to access the records and say a prayer to open the information, accompanied by my guides. The person I was reading for could sometimes resonate with the information that was accessed and confirm their connection to the time period or to the persona that was brought forward.

This has been a wonderful, interactive way to work with the Akashic Records and share information with people. My connection to the records is a work in progress, and new gifts show up every day. I believe I am a keeper of ancestral gifts, and I love bringing these stories forward!

Jennifer Perez Solar

A SERAPHIM ANGEL

I love to work in my Akashic Records every single day. One of the things I find especially joyful is to open my Akashic Records and sit in the beautiful energy of unconditional love. I feel wrapped in the essence of love, which allows me to take time to just *be*. The peace I experience is a lovely way to start the day.

Some days, after infusing my body in peace and love, I say to my record keepers: "Please tell me about a lifetime that I haven't remembered or seen yet."

One foggy day, they replied, *Let's go flying.*

I wasn't sure what they meant, but of course, I agreed. As I sat with my eyes closed and my hand on my heart, I felt myself soaring. At first it felt like a cool, swirling, soft breeze. Then everything became quiet. As we came out of the fog, I realized I was not flying over the Earth.

It felt like I was soaring through the stars! I asked my record keepers if this was a night sky above Earth, and they said *No. You're out among the galaxies.*

Then, in the distance, I saw a planet. As I flew closer, I saw an image of myself standing on this small planet.

Part Two

I was in angelic form. This surprised me, as I never thought of myself as an angel. I asked the record keepers for more information about this aspect of my soul.

They told me that in the early times of my soul, I was a *seraphim angel*.

One of the great gifts of the Akasha is that we often receive information as a clear knowingness called *claircognizance*. As I saw myself in angelic form, standing on this beautiful, small, green world, I knew what the record keepers said was true. I knew on a deeper level who I was. The information that I received was that the *seraphim* came from the twelfth dimension. We became the guardians of the Earth, to protect our Earth timelines until humanity could evolve to the level where we all become the guardians of this planet. That time is now.

This was a new awakening for me. Ever since I was a young child, I could remember the sensation of not being in a physical body. I always wondered why I had come back to Earth this time. I realized through my work in the Akasha that I had come as a whale from Sirius and offered my allegiance to Gaia as an Earth guardian at that time, long ago. Now, I realize that even before I was a whale, I was a 12th-dimensional angel, offering support to humanity at this time in history. I knew that teaching people to access their personal Akasha was part of the support that I came to offer to humanity.

As I watched myself standing there, I saw many beautiful angels flying in from the black, starlit sky surrounding the world on which I stood. I watched as they landed, coming closer as they created a circle around me. Their wings were all touching as if holding hands. I felt their love encircle me completely.

As I stood in awe, in the center of this angelic circle, I started to hear music in my head. They were sending their song telepathically to me. And then I heard these lilting voices sing to me, *We are your Seraphim family*. I could feel soft tears of joy running down my face, as my heart expanded even further.

We stood in this energy of love for a long while. My Seraphim family said to me, *We have traveled from the outer galaxies to gather with you in this moment, our sister.*

They shared memories of our journeys together, throughout the universes. *We are creator beings, angels from Source. Our family has been an aspect in the ethers, knowing its oneness and its creative ability. We have created planets, solar systems, galaxies, and universes. And then, you wanted more, sweet angel sister.*

You wanted more experience... something different and larger than the luminescent beings in the heavens, birthing beautiful worlds and galaxies. You had done this beautiful work with us, our seraphim sister, and then you chose Earth. You have lived on that beautiful, blue-green planet for more than one thousand lifetimes. You have learned, loved, struggled, forgiven, and grown as the infinite soul you are.

Please feel our love as we honor you for your commitment to planet Earth and to humanity. You are brave as well as wise. We are always here with you as you walk the Earth. Your purpose now is to support people to awaken by using their healing gifts as they access greater wisdom. We know this beautiful, yet dense, planet is not always easy to navigate. You often think you are only human—but you and every person on the planet are so much more. You are all Divine beings of love.

Please call upon us often. We love you always.

As I came back from this beautiful journey into the Akasha, I felt different. I now understood, on a deeper level, who I truly am as an infinite, angelic soul. The energy of love and remembrance settled into my cells as I allowed time for my body to integrate into the joy I had experienced.

I am honored to be of service to humanity. Thank you for joining me on this journey.

Lisa Barnett

PART THREE

Deepening Your Experience of the Akasha

Consciousness is a precondition of being.

—CARL JUNG

GUIDED, GUARDED, AND PROTECTED

*H*ave you felt that you need clarification about the next step or choice you want to make? Did you know that most of us are confused about our life paths and our decisions because we have *other people's energy* in our field? That means that others' feelings and thoughts may blend with your own, confusing you.

Most of us are not taught about boundaries, and we might grow up without knowing what our limits could be. Yet, creating clear boundaries and filling your body and energy field with your energy is vital when aligning with your soul's path and purpose. It's also advantageous when we want to receive soul guidance.

The Akashic Record Keepers want us to always feel guided, guarded, and protected. When we walk through our lives connected to soul guidance, we feel safe because we own our energy field and body, knowing our soul and our Akashic Record Keepers are protecting us. One of the easiest ways to maintain that connection is by consciously being sovereign of our physical bodies and energy fields. That means you must be the queen or king of your body by filling up with your personal soul energy every day. You must learn

Part Three

to consciously own the right to have your own space, thoughts, feelings, and desires.

When we become conscious that, although we may appear to be solid matter, we are primarily energy, we realize that we can't start to change unless we know whose energy is in our physical body and energy field.

Imagine your energy field as an empty glass. Every day, you pour a little of yourself in there. Then your mother calls and pours a little of herself into your glass. When your husband asks you to run some errands, your energy glass takes on a bit of his energy. If you have children, and they have requests and needs, their energy is also pouring into the glass. At the end of your day, there you are, with a little bit of your energy and a great deal of other people's energy and desires in your glass. That is exhausting and confusing.

Unknowingly carrying around other people's energy makes us feel burdened and out of sorts. When clients tell me they feel like they have a heavy weight on their shoulders, I know they have filled their glass with everyone's energy except their own.

We assume all our thoughts and feelings belong to us. Sometimes, we need clarification about these feelings because we don't know where they came from. What's most important is to stop for a moment and think about how you feel and whether that feeling really is yours. It can be a relief to realize that not everything we think or feel is ours; our feelings can belong to another. Our work in the Akashic Records helps us sort all this out. We can ask for help to understand what is and what is not ours.

Although it's rarely talked about, our energy fields are open and accessible for other people to tap into. We all share energy unconsciously. But the truth is, especially for empaths, our gates are wide open. We want to make people happy. We willingly take on their problems and their issues. We want to rescue them, and in doing so, we forget about ourselves. Most people don't realize this until they are at the end of their life and they wonder why they never created their desired life. Then they ask, why were we so busy with the needs of others that we forgot about our own needs?

You may wonder why you feel so empty and sad when your children leave home or attend college. You might have dedicated your life to them, which is a great purpose. What isn't conscious is that we let ourselves be filled with their energy and the energy of other moms or teachers. Their expectations and our need to not disappoint them took over our lives. We unconsciously gave our power over by making their purpose more important than ours. Often, others enmesh us so deeply in their energy that we forget what our energy feels like. And the hamster's wheel keeps going around and around.

When we lean into feeling guided, guarded, and protected, we must consciously take ownership of our body and energy field. We are the vessel our soul works through.

ENERGETIC DAMAGE

We might have unconsciously put our bodies and energy into the world without taking steps to protect them. Please don't let these ideas frighten you—awareness and energy tools are the first step to being a sovereign person. When we are unaware, we leave ourselves open. Our physical body, our energy field, and auric field are unprotected and open to energetic attacks.

These include energetic attacks by people who have negative emotions toward us, such as anger, hurt, jealousy, or envy. When we have relationships with people who get upset with us, and then yell or are violent and emotionally abusive, that energy can tear holes in our auric field, making our energy field leaky and therefore open to other energy attacks.

Part Three

ANGRY ENERGY ATTACH

Many years ago, when my three children were toddlers, I drove away from the grocery store with them all lined up in their car seats. I pulled my big van slowly out of the parking lot and onto a small street, as I had done hundreds of times before. On that day, a large truck flew through the intersection and slammed on its brakes, honking its horn, almost hitting my van.

He was speeding through a yellow traffic light and trying to make it through the next one before it turned red. His screeching brakes terrified me as he continued honking his horn at me. Then he pulled up next to me at the next red light, screaming and flipping me off. Again, I was terrified as I looked back at my toddlers in the back seat.

His energy was so intense and violent that even though he was in his car, and I was in mine, I was scared for our lives. I know he ripped a hole in my energy field because my whole body ached while I drove the eight blocks home. My first chakra, which governs survival, felt inflamed. My lower back was in pain. It was such a clear example of how someone's anger can hurt us physically, even without ever touching us.

Not long after, the Akashic Record Keepers gave me a powerful guided meditation to keep me guided, guarded, and protected—which I also call the Rainbow Shield. The record keepers shared with me how essential it was for my well-being to own my own space. They told me to fill my body daily with my highest Akashic energy, light, and physical vibration.

Once my body was full of golden light, I would fill my entire auric field until I looked like a golden egg. Then, on top of that golden energy, I would activate the rainbow shield, which are the layers of the aura. I would then set the intention that no one and nothing could enter my physical body, my energy field, or my auric field without my permission and consent. It was such a beautiful, simple, and profound guided visualization.

Using tools like the rainbow shield, described below, helps you consciously fill your space with your highest energy, vibration, and light. Otherwise, just like the empty glass I used as an example, other people's energy, thoughts, and emotions will fill your body and energy fields. We feel all that energy when we are highly sensitive and empathic.

One of the first steps to accessing your higher guidance and Akashic Records is to be sovereign of your body, energy, and auric fields. This helps you to also be sovereign of your life. When you start owning your whole body and energy field, you consciously bring yourself into this moment and into greater alignment with your Akashic Records.

The guided visualizations from the record keepers make accessing the records more accessible. We all learn that part of the process is learning to be sovereign of our bodies, energetic and physical. That is why we must clear our energy fields, so our magnificent vessel of Source energy can empowered by being guided, guarded, and protected.

Let's take a few minutes and do the Rainbow Shield meditation so you can be guided, guarded, and protected as you walk through your day.

RAINBOW SHIELD GUIDED MEDITATION

We will start by imagining there is a beautiful glass pitcher filled with golden, liquid light floating above your head, just above your crown chakra. Slowly and gently invite your crown chakra to open a little more. Open your crown chakra to receive this beautiful, high vibrational golden energy along with the highest Akashic light and love.

This beautiful, golden, liquid light pours into your crown, flowing down to your feet, filling your feet, your toes, and all the way up your ankles and calves, filling your legs, over your knees, and up into your thighs. Your legs now feel beautifully full of golden energy, moving, clearing, and releasing anything that does not belong in your space, moving anyone and anything out that isn't in the highest and best resonance of you. Then the golden, liquid light continues to fill your torso, moving through your body, your organs, and every area of your body.

The light is filling your stomach and your organs at the etheric levels and layers, as well as the chakras, the channels, as it keeps rising into your lungs, your physical heart, and your fourth chakra. Now it has filled you all the way up to the top of your body.

As the light reaches your shoulders, some of this liquid gold pours down your arms, all the way down to the tips of your fingers, filling and clearing your fingers, your hands, and your arms, clearing and opening the channels in your arms all the way through to the flesh, the bone, and the muscle, filling your arms all the way back up to your shoulders. It continues up into your neck and throat and your fifth chakra, your voice box, on up into your head.

Then it continues to fill and clear your communication levels, your throat, your mouth, your head, and your brain, up into the pineal and the pituitary glands. The light moves people out of your telepathic system and out of your sinuses, out of your eyes, out of your clairaudient channels, out of your ears. Now you own and claim all the space in your whole body, including your head, your third eye, and your clairvoyance.

As the golden liquid light reaches the top of your head, it begins to spill over and around your body. It reaches a foot below your physical feet, filling your whole auric field and your beautiful, egg-shaped aura. And this gold, liquid light rises all around your body, 360 degrees around you. Your feet and your legs slip under this golden light as your aura fills. It rises over your torso, filling all around your body, around your physical body, up around your neck, and around your head, all the way to the very top until it rises about a foot above your head.

Now see or imagine yourself as a beautiful golden egg. The golden, liquid light stops pouring. You are now very solid, filled with your high vibrational energy, the highest energy you can hold. The energy fills you from the inside, moving out to the edge of your aura. You've moved everyone else out of your space. And now we're going to add one more layer of naturally occurring protection.

Imagine this as a seven-layered rainbow. It's all the colors of your chakras, from red to orange; add yellow, green, blue, indigo, and the gorgeous violet. And the seven layers of this rainbow cover your whole auric field. They are your natural auric layers, always there for you. Now the beautiful golden egg that surrounds you is wrapped in this magnificent rainbow protection all the way around you, from the bottom of your feet to the top of your head. See the rainbow going out, wrapping around from front to back until it extends about a foot around your whole body.

And now you are solid golden light from your core to the edge of your aura, encased in the seven layers of your rainbow. So let us activate and empower your protection with these words: *Nothing may enter my energy field and body without my permission, and nothing may be taken, depleted, or removed from my body and field without my permission.*

We have activated a vital shield for you, so that no one can take your energy from you, because no one and nothing can penetrate this beautiful, golden, shielded egg.

When you start doing the rainbow shield meditation daily, you will feel more aligned to your soul's path because you've moved other people and their energy out of your field. You may even find that your thoughts, mental chatter, and feelings change. For example, you might feel a depression lift because it never belonged to you, or you may find yourself naturally thinking happy or positive thoughts because the old, angry, or stressful thoughts weren't yours. This meditation is like a magic wand, protecting you with a golden shield repelling outside influences.

Part Three

YOU HAVE UNIQUE GIFTS

Many people wonder if they have the ability or gifts to access their Akashic Records. *How will the energy come through? If I'm not clairvoyant, will I get information?*

You are a unique soul, and each of you will receive soul information differently. Consider that you are a blend of 500 or 800 lifetimes here on Earth. You have your unique combination of those numerous lifetimes where you have honed various skills and talents. You start each life with a different soul plan, building on your unique combinations of experiences.

No two people can have the same personal gifts or how they use them. Remember, everything is energy, and we each vibrate at different frequencies. We may have similar gifts but not the same ones.

One person will have experience as an intuitive in this life, along with ten past lifetimes as an intuitive. Another person may be working in the corporate world but have many other lifetimes as a healer and might want to become a healer again in this life. That could look like working in a human resources position, where your job considers the well-being of every employee. A third person might be an artist creating high vibrational art which helps other people raise their vibration by displaying beauty in their homes. A fourth person might have had a contract with the dead as a child, before they got scared and turned that gift off. And a fifth person is a third-generation psychic with ancestral and past-life gifts.

Each of these people will have a different life plan and a different way to connect with Akashic information.

If your gifts have something to do with healing, that does not mean your work in the world must be in the healing arts. You can employ your talents and natural skills at work, home, or business. The focus doesn't have to be healing or intuition; it is being aware of our gifts and using them when dealing with people at a higher vibration. Your intention to raise the vibration of your world leads your every action and decision, no matter where you find yourself.

Our soul's plan is a compilation of gifts we want to use garnered from our developed skills in other lifetimes, including our genetic gifts from our family. We have a variety of abilities such as clairvoyance, clairaudience, claircognizance, and clairsentience.

People who are clairsentient can feel a lot of energy moving in their bodies and around them. However, since they may also be very empathic and sensitive, their energy field can be overrun with other people's energy. This will affect how they receive information.

Clairvoyants may see clearly, receiving a lot of images or occasionally a short movie. Clairaudients hear rather than see or feel. Many of my students expect to hear a loud, imposing voice outside themselves—yet most of us experience these communications as a quiet, loving voice that sounds like our own voice inside our mind. Working with the Akashic Records becomes about deciphering what they hear and deciding whether it is coming from the ego or the soul. They start to ask: *Is this me thinking something, or is it a clairaudient message from the record keepers?*

Clairaudient messages often have a different tonality. They might use grammar and vocabulary the person hearing them wouldn't use, or the information may appear to have a noticeable cadence. One of the things I want to share with you is how vital it is to receive the information without judgment. Journal what you're thinking and hearing, then go back to read the message later. That is when you will notice more easily if the message is from you or from the records.

When we read that message again, we often feel emotional, because we realize it is a clairaudient message from our Akashic Record Keepers. But, as I mentioned earlier, everyone can access the Akashic Records. We only need the time and practice to understand how best we receive this information.

Journaling while in our Akashic Records helps us to get out of the way without fear that nothing will come through. Of course, when we worry if any information will come through, we're not allowing the energy of the Akasha to flow to us. As a student, you are building your abilities to become aligned with your soul's information, which takes time and patience. Then comes confidence and clarity as you become proficient using the access prayer and formulating questions.

Practicing also helps us move past self-doubt. Doubt is a significant detriment to soul work for many people. Please don't let it stop you from starting on this profound journey.

HEALING PRAYERS

The record keepers have given me many healing prayers. The beauty of these prayers is that they were channeled from the Divine and imbued with healing Akasha energy. The Akashic Record Keepers gave me two energetic types of prayers to teach. One is the Akasha Access Prayer, a vibrational key to move you into union with your Akashic library and Akashic Record Keepers.

The second is the Akashic Healing Prayers, which I've channeled from the Akasha to help humanity heal trauma on many levels. These healing prayers are helpful for daily use as they clear our energy field and help with many of our fears. My second book, *From Questioning to Knowing: 73 Prayers to Transform Your Life* includes many prayers you can share with family and friends. They are short and simple, yet potent.

One of my favorite prayers to assist in creating clearer boundaries is the Prayer to Clear Other People's Energy. It is the fastest way to clear our energy field of other people's stuff as we learn to be sovereign of our space and body. As I mentioned earlier, releasing people's energy from our bodies and energy field is vital when doing our inner work.

Here it is. Let's say the prayer now. Repeat it three times to really activate its energy.

PRAYER TO CLEAR OTHER PEOPLE'S ENERGY

> Mother, Father, Goddess God, please assist me in clearing and releasing all outside energies that are in my body and energy field. Please send them back to the person from whom they came or send them to Divine Source to be recycled for the highest good of all. I am filled with my purest energy and the highest vibrations I can now hold. So it is.

Use this prayer before you do your Rainbow Shield Meditation, to help you clear your body and auric field, and before you fill yourself with your highest Akashic gold energy, soul vibration, and light. It's a perfect way to start having sovereignty over your body.

OVERCOMING KARMIC PATTERNS

We discussed soul contracts with karma attached in earlier chapters, so let's go deeper into healing those attachments. In soul planning, we choose different challenges, which I often call "karmic patterns" because these challenges usually repeat over many lifetimes. The soul wants us to become aware they are patterns so we can stop repeating them. Our karmic patterns were written into our soul plans because we must strengthen these areas to fulfill our soul's mission. And before we can find our strengths, transforming challenges is essential.

These different karmic patterns appear in many areas of our lives but look and feel different, including their intensity. Our spiritual journey entails looking at our challenges as opportunities for self-actualization and self-discovery, as well as finding the hidden talents or skills the karmic lesson had camouflaged. By changing how we face adversity, we take victimization out of the experience and can become empowered by it. We start to see the bigger picture. The more aware we become of repeated patterns in our lives and relationships, the faster we heal the karmic lesson to get on with living a loving life.

Part of the spiritual path is understanding compassion and forgiveness and trusting ourselves enough to apply it. The record keepers tell us that forgiveness heals karma. It is genuinely a choice for us as expansive souls who desire to learn and grow in wisdom.

Many souls choose to be born into families with extremely complex dynamics to overcome, such as patterns of abuse, addiction, and abandonment. Because these are so deeply rooted in our sense of self, finding self-love is a challenge. We pick these families for various reasons, to break free of the shame and guilt of living in a family with so many karmic patterns.

If we take our humanness out for a moment to observe from the soul's perspective, we may all come together in a family unit to support one or more people within our family. But of course, we don't remember the original intention. Nonetheless, we have an understanding to play the agreed-upon roles.

There are so many levels of karmic patterns to overcome. It is hard to say what is difficult for one soul may not be so for another. As I have mentioned, our paths are unique to what we came here to accomplish. And because we are ancient, wise, and powerful souls, we want to help soul family members evolve into love. It doesn't seem problematic from a soul level, but once we put our human body suit on and the ego is active, many of these patterns can seem insurmountable, because we really expect a lot from ourselves. We have no memory of our soul's lofty goals for our human form.

Earlier, I gave you an example of how souls agree to incarnate into a family with alcoholic and abusive patterns. Looking at the soul contracts between parents, they chose to be with each other to discover a way to heal their emotional and psychological wounds that support destructive patterns. The alcoholic parent may have contracted with the abusive parent to treat them poorly and to keep drinking excessively as a distraction. Their soul may be ready to let go of feeling unworthy, guilty, and shameful, but the inner turmoil is too intense for them to feel strong enough to leave the relationship and stop drinking. So, the patterns continue, and they're stuck, going into another lifetime carrying the burden of the karmic patterns until they get it right by finding love for themselves.

From the abusive adult's perspective, their contract had them continue to play the abusive role until the alcoholic found the strength to change their ways. Since the alcoholic isn't changing, the abusive adult has a choice. Do they stay stuck in being an abusive partner or leave the relationship? They will have to leave the relationship if they let go of being mean, to embrace worthiness and learn about kindness to themself. They must leave that life behind and be on a conscious, healing path to avoid attracting another addiction-prone partner.

ENDING ABUSE

What I find exciting is that at this time in history, there is a massive collective contract on Earth to end abuse for all of humanity. Many souls have taken on the tough job of being born into families where they will experience different levels and variations of abuse. They have chosen to write soul contracts with families to end the destructive patterns passed down by generations. Their soul agrees to complete it in their lifetime by not passing it down to their

Part Three

own children. Just look at the generations in the last few decades. They are consciously raising their children differently than their parents raised them.

Many of these children of abuse go on and consciously choose to teach their children how to feel compassion and share their feelings. Parents teach them the vocabulary of emotions to talk about their feelings and help them learn words to explain themselves.

Those generations feel compassion and love for themselves and the families they choose to build. They love their children without the anger, malice, or the abusive pattern their parents unconsciously or consciously demonstrated. In setting solid boundaries, the new generations of souls are stopping abuse patterns and removing them from their own ancestral lineage.

The Akashic Record Keepers know of the difficult path these beautiful souls have taken by choosing to be part of that collective, passing on their unconditional love and gratitude. It is a brave journey and a significant job they do for humanity. These courageous souls said, "Let us do this… because we can." If you are one of them… *Thank you.*

The record keepers talk about how important it is for humans to feel safe, especially in dangerous situations such as drug addiction or abuse. They suggest finding a place or person where you feel safe, where you can talk about what you're thinking or feeling about life in a household with an alcoholic or an abuser. Feeling safe may happen in therapy. Often forgiveness comes much later.

Because of all the soul learning you received from living in your household, your soul path may be to share what you have learned with other people by becoming their therapists. Someone else may choose to be a healer and share what they have learned through their healing practice. Or you may continue to work on healing yourself and never share it except with one or two people you realize need that information to help them find forgiveness.

Or you can just be living your life, doing the things you love, and working at your job—and because you have done so much healing work on yourself, your heart and soul are putting out high-vibrational energy to heal those in your field of energy. You are healing others without even knowing who you may be helping. That is also healing from a soul level.

The record keepers remind us often that there is no right or wrong way to complete karmic patterns. Instead, our paths are about learning and experiencing life for soul growth and raising our vibration to affect those who can't do it for themselves.

It's not about how we do it—although unfortunately, sometimes we have that soul contract and must complete our side of the agreement to move on, because our parents or partners are not interested in going to therapy or rehab or even speaking about their pain. It is their choice, according to the record keepers; it isn't right or wrong. It is simply the path they chose.

Our loving librarians want us to know that completing our side of the contract frees us from that karmic pattern for good. All the various beings of light and the record keepers greatly respect us for coming into human form with all the challenges and struggles this dimension holds. In this world, they honor us with unconditional love and light.

Now is the time to forgive yourself and all others that have harmed you and be free of the energy of the past.

FORGIVENESS AS A PATH TO AWAKENING

I would like to share the Prayer of Forgiveness that the Akashic Record Keepers have given us. Forgiveness is not only a way to clear karma, but also a path to awakening. When you move from anger and judgment to compassion and forgiveness, you are shifting your consciousness to a higher vibration. The vibration of love and forgiveness is on the way to the vibration of enlightenment.

PRAYER OF FORGIVENESS

Divine, Spirit, Source, please move me into a state of forgiveness toward anyone or anything that has hurt me, consciously or unconsciously, from the beginning of time to this present moment. I now forgive them, and I release the energy of the past.

Divine, Spirit, Source, please move me into a state of forgiveness toward myself for any hurt that I have caused others, consciously or unconsciously, from the beginning of time to this present moment. I now forgive myself and I release the energy of the past.

Divine, Spirit, Source, please move me into a state of forgiveness for any hurt I have caused myself, consciously or unconsciously, from the beginning of time to this present moment. I now forgive myself and release the energy of the past.

I invoke the grace and power of forgiveness to transform my body, mind, and heart as I return to Divine innocence. And so it is, with gratitude.

The record keepers suggest we say the Forgiveness Prayer at least once a day for thirty-three days. Working with this prayer for thirty-three days consecutively has the power to heal chasms of pain and separation in relationships with self, Source, other people, and situations in our lives.

Forgiveness clears karma throughout time and space. It allows us to heal our past, which consists of anything prior to this moment and includes our childhood and past lives. When done at the end of the day, the prayer helps to clear up all the negativity that builds within us.

When we learn to create clear boundaries for ourselves by using tools like the Rainbow Shield, moving others out of our space with the clearing prayers we've learned, and starting our forgiveness work, we align with higher vibrations. We are beginning the process of creating the life our soul desires.

In the next chapter, you will learn more tools to call back some of your scattered energy and other guided visualizations to support your soul growth.

EMBODYING THE AKASHA

As we grow spiritually, it is a good idea to start accessing Divine wisdom to receive information with clarity about who you are and who you have been in other lifetimes. In the Akasha, we can even learn about different dimensions. This is because we are infinite souls with thousands of lifetimes.

Moving forward in this time in history, we can rely on our soul guidance from the Akasha as we embark on the paths before us. We can do this in a few different ways.

OTHER WAYS TO ACCESS THE AKASHIC RECORDS

People access the Akashic Records in various ways; one such way is learning to meditate to access the quantum field of the Akasha. However, that can take many years and intense meditation practice.

I have seen some people practice dowsing, hoping that they're accessing their guidance through the Akashic Records. In dousing, you ask various yes or no questions to get clear answers. But it's easy for the mind and ego to take over your intuition when using this method, especially if you're new to dowsing.

You can also use gemstones, colors, jewelry, and artwork to assist you in creating a more profound connection when accessing the Akashic Records.

Some people, including myself, offer guided meditations that take you into the records. These meditations can feel wonderful and are heart-opening. The most significant drawback is that you can't communicate with your record keepers in these meditations.

Try different ways to access and deepen your connection with your librarians. Find the ways that give you the best connection to the unconditional love waiting for you within your soul's records.

The most straightforward and direct process I've found is to use a sacred vibration key to open the Akasha, such as the Five-Step Wisdom Prayer System you will learn in the next chapter. With that process, you will learn to move into your record and will be able to communicate with your record keepers.

First, let's start with getting into your body and grounded.

THE IMPORTANCE OF BEING GROUNDED

Grounding is a profound process for many reasons. First, most people are unconscious of where their energy is going. They might resist being in the body because it can feel heavy, dense, and emotional, unpleasant sensations for many people. It's much denser than we're used to as light beings. Learning to ground yourself will change your life.

Two important benefits of being grounded include: It puts you in the present moment, so you're not living in the past or future and it helps to manifest what you need to create your most aligned life.

Unless you're in the present moment and entirely in your body, creating your desired outcome in life is a challenge. All our intentions are just that—

intentions—unless we have the physical level of energy and connection to our earthly plane to manifest our desires and dreams now.

GUIDED VISUALIZATIONS TO SUPPORT YOUR SOUL GROWTH

One of the Akashic Record Keepers' gifts is guided visualizations. These energy tools work in a variety of ways that are helpful for people on a spiritual path.

The first tool will assist you in grounding yourself and being more present in your body, which makes it easier to access the records.

In the second tool, we reclaim our life force energy by calling back the energy left scattered around the world. This is important as we raise our vibration and become more fully and consciously embodied.

Finally, in the third visualization, we will create a powerful Akashic column of light around ourselves, connecting us to the Akasha. This extra connection layer is helpful as we learn to access our personal Akashic Records.

You might want to read the written words into a recorder and play it back while doing the guided visualization.

TRIPOD GROUNDING SYSTEM GUIDED VISUALIZATION

Let's start with your feet flat on the floor, sitting comfortably in a chair with your eyes closed. Imagine you're moving out of your head and down into your heart center. Taking a few deep breaths, feel your heart opening and expanding.

Now we invite your soul to fully come into your physical body. Feel your beautiful energy coming down into your crown chakra as it fills your head, down into your upper torso, your heart, and lungs, and down into your midsection.

Take another deep, expansive breath as you invite your soul to come more fully down into your lower abdomen and hips. Take a moment to feel how grounded you are when your soul is down in your torso, filling your hips. Now imagine that energy continuing down into your thighs, calves, and feet.

You will now activate your tripod grounding system by visualizing that you have a root system from the bottom of your feet extending deep down into the Earth. The roots go down three feet, four feet, even five feet, and then they spread out, creating an extensive root system below your body.

With your root system complete, you come back into the first chakra. Let's grow a wide tail or grounding cord that begins at the base of your spine and goes all the way down and around the crystalline core of our dear Mother Earth.

Taking a moment to feel how this tripod grounding system feels as it comes from your two feet and your grounding cord, making you feel solidly connected to the Earth and truly grounded and held in love in your physical body.

Taking another deep breath as you notice what that feels like for you. When you're ready, open your eyes, fully grounded and embodied in the present.

CALL BACK YOUR ENERGY

One of the most powerful tools I offer my students is a guided visualization that helps them call back their energy. We leave our energy scattered around the world without even realizing it. For example, when we travel to a beautiful place, we often feel reluctant to leave. The desirous part of us that wants to stay there inadvertently leaves an energic part of us behind to sustain a connection. When we talk on the phone with our friends and family, go to meetings, or work, we are leaving parts of our energy behind with each meaningful encounter. You might even leave a piece of your energy behind if you've had a heated discussion or argument with somebody, just by continuing to be upset or angry.

There is a flip side to leaving your energy behind, such as when you had a fabulous time at a gathering. Continuing to think about it, remembering, or reminiscing also leaves bits of you behind. Imagine how draining the cumulative effect of leaving small pieces of your energy scattered over a lifetime would be.

Sometimes, we can feel people in different areas of our bodies. For instance, the telepathic channels around your eyes coincide with your sinuses. When you think you're getting a stuffy nose from the weather change, it might be because someone is thinking about you and conversing with you in their mind. You would be surprised how often you unconsciously leave your energy connected to other people and places. This can cause a feeling of fragmentation, as if somehow you are not whole. You can't quite put your finger on it, but you are not 100 percent present.

So, let's get started on reclaiming your energy. You will feel wonderfully full of yourself, in a good way.

CALLING BACK YOUR ENERGY MEDITATION

Start with three deep breaths.

For the first one, fill your whole body from the tips of your toes all the way up to the top of your head. Exhale deeply and completely.

For your second breath, fill your belly until it expands fully, hold it for a moment, then exhale slowly.

Your third breath will focus on your heart area as you allow your heart to open and expand to breathe in peace and joy. Exhale to release anything that no longer serves you at that moment or stops you from experiencing the peace and joy you just breathed into your heart.

Part Three

Next, soften your eyes as you let your body relax in your chair and invite your spirit to come fully down into your physical body. Feel the Divine support all around you as you connect to dear Mother Earth beneath your feet. Activate your Tripod Grounding System, from the prior visualization. Thank the Earth for supporting you as you walk on her daily, going forward on your journey.

It can be grounding to go outside and walk barefoot on the grass or on the sand at the beach. Do whatever you can to connect and enjoy the Earth beneath your feet.

Now imagine a big, golden sun about the size of a basketball hovering above your head. Invite the sun to start spinning. Set the intention that as the golden sun is spinning and spinning, it is calling back your very own energy – all the energy you have left scattered around the world.

Imagine this golden sphere continuing to magnetically attract your energy back to you as it spins above your head. It is above your crown chakra and calling back all the positive and loving scattered energy you had left behind. That energy is merging with that golden sun. Take a moment and notice how this feels.

Let the big, golden ball spin, breathing deeply, feeling and picturing that energy returning. The golden sun is pulling back your energy as though it is a magnet. As the spinning slows, the sun becomes beautiful, golden liquid sunlight pouring into your crown chakra.

As your energy flows into your body, it becomes converted into the highest and best golden vibration of you, returning home to the highest levels in your body, your energy field, and your auric field. It returns to wherever it came from. It returns to the best place for it to go; you do not have to figure out where it should go.

Feel your precious energy returning to you. It may feel like warmth dripping right through your body, or you might notice the energy as a tingle running all the way down into your toes. It is the highest energy of you, returning home to you now.

COLUMN OF LIGHT MEDITATION

The Akashic Record Keepers offer this visual meditation to assist in connecting to them by surrounding yourself with this Akashic Column of Light. Use this visualization to assist in grounding the Akashic energy to Earth as you wrap yourself in its light. This is perfect to do after you open your Akashic Records using the upcoming Five-Step Wisdom Prayer System.

Please start by closing your eyes. Keep your feet flat on the floor. Focus on your connection to your dear mother Earth who rests solidly beneath your feet. Bring your focus from your feet slowly up to your heart, always breathing deeply into your heart.

See your heart open, ever-expanding. Relax into the expansion, allowing your heart to fill with unconditional love. Stay there until you feel it fully. Breathe into the continued expansion of your heart.

Now move your attention and the energy up into your head. Focus on the area between your eyebrows moving back into the center of your head. There you will see or feel a small master gland, your pineal gland. Spend time focusing on this part of your body and sending it love.

Thank it for all the work it does to assist your body. Send love from your heart to your pineal gland, for it is the energy center that connects to your higher self, your soul, and eventually to the Keepers of the Akashic Records and your Akashic Masters. Your connection is how we can communicate with you.

See and feel the energy flow from Earth up through your feet. Let it rise into your heart and move up to connect your heart to your pineal gland. Pay attention to energy rising from your pineal gland to the top of your head, your crown chakra. Now let the energy continue up from your crown chakra to the twelfth chakra above your head, the place where your higher self resides. Continue the energy flow up from the twelfth chakra and flowing upward to connect with us in the Akasha.

Imagine a silvery blue column of light coming back down from us to connect to you. The column surrounds your whole body and continues down into the Earth. The Akashic Column of Light that your record keepers and beings of light have sent you surrounds and protects you. Inside this column of light, you are held in Divine love.

Take a few moments to feel your connection to unconditional love or behold the spectacular sight of yourself surrounded and protected in the silvery blue column. Take a moment to breathe in and feel the unconditional love. Know that you have always been guided.

Inside this connection, you can transform your life with the healing prayers of the Akashic Records. Relax into the healing energy as you recite the prayers. Feel their source energy running through you, surrounding you, filling you with lasting love.

When you feel complete, you may go about your day or you may continue by asking questions in your Akashic Records.

HOW OFTEN DO I USE VISUALIZATIONS?

Practice with these new tools regularly. Grounding every day, or even multiple times a day, is important for most people. Ground yourself if you feel spacey or unable to focus. Try calling back your energy weekly or more often, if you are around a lot of people every day. You can use the column of light daily and journal the information you receive when encircled in the loving Akashic energy.

Practicing the visualization tools on a regular basis will help you to raise your vibration and to align with greater ease into the Akasha. I look forward to leading you through the Five-Step Wisdom Prayer system in the next chapter. You will start to access your own Akashic Records and receive information and guidance from your Akashic Record Keepers.

START ACCESSING YOUR RECORDS

In writing what I know about the Akasha and its books of recordings, I remember the journey I've been on to access and teach about the Akasha. I'd love to share some of it, to help you understand this work's depth and importance.

The Akashic Record Keepers asked me to start a school. Being a curious soul, I needed to understand why they chose me to assist with bringing this wisdom back to humanity. I didn't even know if it was the right thing to do. I was busy raising small children and feeling overwhelmed.

I asked them, "Why me?"

They told me I was a galactic soul and could help many people by bringing a variety of different Akashic access prayers to the world. This would allow more people to gain access to the Akasha. They said that now was the time to make it easier for humanity to gain soul knowledge, and that by consciously accessing the energy of the Akasha, more deliberate healing and transformation would take place.

Before I discovered the conscious prayer process, I would spontaneously go into the energy of the Akasha, but I didn't know where I was or if I was even supposed to be there. When I meditated, I would see the Akasha library guarded by gilded gates.

As I learned, through years of work in my own Akashic Records, one of my contracts with humanity and the record keepers is to share the most conscious and quickest way to access your soul and its record keepers.

I'm happy you heard the call and are joining us in this empowering way.

CREATING YOUR HEART'S DESIRE

Consider why your heart has called you to pick up and read a book about the Akasha. Please spend a few moments thinking about it and then write down what you think the answers may be. The heart and soul work in unison, helping us connect with both as we step onto this unfamiliar path.

When you combine the high-vibrational Akasha energy with the vibration of your heart's desires, you are helping us ground the Akasha's energy here in physical form. It becomes much easier to manifest your desires. Remember, the Akasha is part of the unmanifest energy field where the universe assists us to magnetize and create our desires. Everything is complete in the Akasha.

To manifest our desires, we must let go of the old patterns which limit our ability to vibrate at a frequency of love and abundance. Your Akashic Record work will accelerate the process.

So please take a moment to consider what your heart wants you to ask in your Akashic Record. Do you want to clear out past karma with a friend? Resolve an issue with a family member? Deal with a health concern? Think of a few areas in which you want to receive guidance.

ASKING QUESTIONS IN YOUR AKASHIC RECORD

Your Akashic Record is a vast, infinite field, so learning how to build a theme into your questions becomes critical. There is an art to formulating your questions, and it takes practice. You will receive information that can help you to take steps forward and to make choices that are in your highest and best interests. Yes-or-no questions offer only simple answers, so continually reframe your queries for more depth of information.

Here's an example of the importance of asking the right questions. I had a client who came to me for an Akashic Record consultation. She had been divorced for about three years and was ready for a new relationship, so her questions revolved around that: "Will I have a new boyfriend? When will a new relationship start?"

I'd been working with her for about a year, and she continued to ask these questions. One time she asked, "When, when, when? When will I meet a guy?"

I immediately saw an image. It looked like a Polaroid picture of a man. It was startling to me because it was so specific, right down to the man's hairstyle, including a little bald patch, his red-and-black plaid shirt, and his black pickup truck. I said, "Wow, this is astonishing, it's just like a real photo of somebody. I rarely see that."

We were both excited about this information. She kept asking when she would meet her man. The answer I received for her was, *Within the next two months, and this is what he's going to look like.*

About three weeks later, she called me and said, "I met him. And he looks just like the image you shared."

A few weeks later she called me again. This time it was to complain that the guy was just looking for someone to take care of him and wasn't spiritual at all. She said, "Why did they tell me about this person? He's not who I wanted!"

When I asked the record keepers why this was true, they responded, *You asked when you would meet a man—not a spiritual, kind, and supportive man. It's important to always be consciously aware of what you are asking for.*

It is essential to ask specific questions. If you want a partner to walk your spiritual path and support you, it's okay to ask for it. As you work in your Akashic Record, think about what is truly important to you and how you will ask your questions. Also, think about what your intention is and what kind of energy is behind your questions.

CREATE A NEW HABIT

The Akashic Record Keepers have told us to start creating "Heaven on Earth" daily. That means opening your record every day. Create a daily habit, because this process works when you integrate it as part of your spiritual growth practice. Practice opening your record to receive information with your eyes open.

In the exercise below, I will walk you through opening your own record—but first, you will feel the energy of the access prayer *outside* of the Akashic Record. You will learn to ask your questions both outside and inside your record. Notice the difference in the power of the energy and the answers you receive and in the depth of information.

Write questions about your heart's desires, such as, "How can I fulfill my desire? What is holding me back from having, creating, or receiving my heart's desire? Is there a higher or better intention for me?" Those are perfect questions to ask first *outside* your record and then *inside* your record. With this process, you will begin to dig deep into its energy to experience direct knowledge.

FIVE SIMPLE STEPS

Many years ago, when the Akashic Record Keepers asked me to start an Akashic school, they told me that accessing our own Akashic Records is everyone's birthright. They said they would give me both access prayers and healing prayers, as well as simple steps to support my students. Over the years, that process has turned into my Five-Step Wisdom Prayer System.

I appreciate tools that are simple and concise. When they gave me the outline for teaching the Five-Step Wisdom Prayer System, I loved the combination of linear and spiritual aspects. It aligned with my understanding of how people learn. Using five simple steps in a straightforward way made the process, which often seems complicated, much easier for students to comprehend. It took away the fear of whether they could access the Akasha.

This system of opening your sacred Akashic Records will guide you on a profound journey of information, knowledge, and wisdom. Of course, you also will be healing your body, mind, and emotions. Each time you open your records, this method allows you to do it quickly and maximize your experience. Consistent practice helps you grow in confidence while sharpening your ability to receive channeled information from the Akasha.

The five-step process below comes from my first book, *The Infinite Wisdom of the Akashic Records*.

1. Set your intention for clarity in the guidance you receive.
2. Write out specific questions you want to ask your record keepers. Pick one area at a time to start.
3. Use the given Akashic Access Prayer to open your Akashic Records. Then ask your questions.
4. After completing the questions, fill yourself up with Akashic healing energy and light.
5. Close and lock your records for now.

BE MINDFUL WHEN WORKING IN YOUR RECORDS

Before we start, here are a few guidelines for accessing your own Akashic Record.

- Use your first, middle, and last legal name to open your Akashic Record. Always read the prayer. You do not need to memorize it. Be deliberate in your quest for answers, as it deepens your reception of the information.
- Write three to five questions on one area you wish to work with today. When we ask questions, it gives us accountability for the answers we seek. And wanting to know how to overcome a situation or learn from a karmic lesson demonstrates integrity in our path.
- Please do not teach these Akashic Record prayers to anyone else. Our teachers undergo rigorous training to ensure they have integrity and accountability in deciding to whom they teach these simple, yet potent, Access Prayers.
- Open your Akashic Record daily for the next month and write about your experience in a journal. You will be surprised at how much information you receive during this time.
- Be sure not to use alcohol and drugs, which lower your vibration. I suggest refraining from opening your record until any substance has had time to clear out of your body completely, usually eight to twelve hours. Prescription medications are acceptable, although painkillers and sleeping aids will also lower your vibration and make it harder to access these high-vibrational realms.
- Please do not drive a car with your record open. Working with your record can be distracting and will take your focus off driving or performing other tasks.

OUTSIDE THE AKASHIC RECORDS

I like to start my students out by using the access prayer without opening their records, so they can feel the difference in the energy inside and outside their records. Be sure to have a journal handy to take notes. You will first read the prayer as the directions state below, answer the questions, make notes in your journal, then move on to the Five-Step Akashic Knowing Wisdom Prayer Process.

1. Read the Access prayer once.

SACRED ACCESS PRAYER

Akashic Record Keepers of Unconditional Love, help me to center fully in this moment as I create this sacred space. Please wrap me in your love and allow me to travel to the highest realms of the Akasha available to me today.

Lords, Masters, and Teachers, I ask that you show me what it feels like to be a clear channel of my Akashic Record.

Akashic Beings of Light, please guide me to the deepest truth of me. Support me in healing and releasing the appropriate karma and contracts that have brought me to this life. I give great thanks for your Divine love, support, and protection on this journey.

2. Now answer the following questions:

   a. How does my body feel when I read this prayer?
   b. Is there an emotional connection to this prayer? Do I feel it in my heart or gut?
   c. What am I thinking? Where does my mind go?
   d. Do I receive any images or pictures from this life or other lifetimes with this prayer?

3. Write what you feel, receive, and experience in your journal.

What did you notice? The idea was for you to receive an intuitive feeling and a bit of information about the prayer.

Next, you will learn the detailed steps to go into the Akashic Record. This exercise allows you to feel the difference between your intuition's energy and the energy when accessing the Akasha. Because every person is unique and resonates with different vibrations and information, the prayer feels different for everyone.

Through the years, I've been given eight access prayers to help people interested in working in the Akasha. The record keepers offer new prayers as the energies of the students and the planet continue to upgrade in this beautiful time of shift.

Journaling about your experiences and any information you receive will serve your process well. You are documenting your self-healing journey through your writing. Journaling is one of the most powerful tools to help you empower yourself as you step toward personal change. It will help you grow into your mission for being here as well as evolve in all your relationships. Write about any insights you received after you were in your record. This all adds to awareness on your journey.

Please take a moment to center and ground yourself before you open your Akashic Record. You can use the Tripod Grounding System you learned in the last chapter. Doing so makes it much easier to be in the expansive space of your records, because your body feels connected to Earth and comfortable.

THE AKASHIC KNOWING FIVE-STEP WISDOM PRAYER SYSTEM

You will now learn the system that The Akashic Knowing School of Wisdom teaches to open your sacred Akashic Records. The following serves as a template for every journey you take into your own Akashic Records. Each time you open the records, follow the process to maximize your experience and grow your confidence in your ability to receive channeled information.

Step 1: Set Your Intention

It is vital to be clear and open to the wisdom and healing of the Akashic Records. Begin your time with the Akashic Records by setting your intention to be a pure and perfect channel for yourself. The following prayer will assist you.

PRAYER FOR INTENTION FOR CLARITY

> Akashic Record Keepers, please help me to remove what no longer serves me, including all hidden beliefs, prejudices, outdated patterns, programs, blocks, and constrictions, as I access Akashic Record information for myself today with clarity. I am here to do the work of the Divine. I am clear of other people's energy, and I am full of Divine energy. Information moves freely to me and through me.

Step 2: Write Your Questions

It's important to write several questions around your chosen topic before you open your Akashic Record. The more questions you ask, the deeper the answer and broader the perspective you will receive from your Akashic Records. You may have several questions already in mind before you open your records. Take a moment to clarify what it is that you really seek to know. If you get stuck, ask a couple of yes/no questions to ensure you are in the records.

For this first venture into the Akasha, I recommend starting with some simple questions as you get the feel of this work. Some suggestions are:

- How can I best use the Akashic Record today or in my life?
- How can I be of service to myself, my community, or my family?
- Is there any exercise or food that would be beneficial for me today?
- What would my Beings of Light like me to know about today?

Step 3: Open Your Records Using the Sacred Access Prayer

To open your record read the prayer out loud once, as it is written. Then repeat the prayer two times silently, inserting your current legal name where the capitalized and bolded ME/MY are. Your current legal name is the first, middle, and last name that appears on your driver's license or passport. If you do not have a middle name, that is fine.

Notice how your body feels when you read this prayer. Do you feel this prayer in your heart or your gut? Do you feel an emotional attachment to the prayer? Take notes. Please remember to read the prayer aloud once and silently twice with your legal name in place of ME/MY.

SACRED ACCESS PRAYER

Akashic Record Keepers of Unconditional Love, help me to center fully in this moment as I create this sacred space. Please wrap me in your love and allow me to travel to the highest realms of the Akasha available to ME today.

Lords, Masters, and Teachers, I ask that you show me what it feels like to be a clear channel of MY Akashic Record.

Akashic Beings of Light, please guide me to the deepest Truth of ME. Support me in healing and releasing the appropriate karma and contracts that have brought me to this life. I give great thanks for your Divine love, support, and protection on this journey.

Allow yourself to take a few breaths and sink deeply into the energy of the records. Once you feel the records are open, begin to ask the simple questions you have written out. Start journaling and recording all the information you receive. Remember, it may be subtle energy in the form of tingles or swirling, as well as words, thoughts, images, and knowing.

Some days, you may spend thirty minutes working in the records, asking questions; other days, you might be surprised that an hour flies by as you deepen your understanding of who you are as a human being with many gifts and talents, soul contracts, and challenges to understand. Take your time to learn and ensure clarity on each of the steps.

Step 4: Fill Yourself Up with Your Highest Energy

Do this at any time during your session after you have received clearing or healing from your record keepers, or when you are nearing the end of your time in the Akashic Records. Remember that you do not need to do specific healing to do this step. Just being in your records, receiving wisdom that helps to realign you to your soul's path, is incredibly healing.

PRAYER TO FILL UP WITH HIGHEST AKASHIC ENERGY

Please fill me up with my highest and best Akashic Record information and the highest and best physical level energy and information I can now hold. Thank you for your healing today.

Part Three

Step 5: Close your Akashic Records

The fifth step is about completion. We thank the Akashic Record Keepers for the love, wisdom, and healing we have received. Then we close and lock our Akashic Records. Ending the session with gratitude and closure is important so you can go on with the rest of your day, feeling complete and ready to bring your new understanding, unconditional love, and wisdom out into your world.

When you feel complete, use the following prayer to close your records.

AKASHIC RECORDS CLOSING PRAYER

> Thank you, dear Beings of Light, for the unconditional love, the wisdom, the information, and the healing I have received today.
>
> Please help me to return fully into my complete human wholeness, in all dimensions, times, and planes. Please help me to integrate the information and healing received with ease and grace.
>
> I ask that you close and lock the records of (*insert your legal name*). And so it is. Amen, Amen, Amen.

PRACTICE OPENING YOUR RECORDS

Each time you use the access prayer, your energetic vibration rises. The first time you open your records, you step into the Akasha realm by opening the door to your records. You will start to go deeper the second and third times, and before you know it, you will have built a relationship with your record keepers.

These prayers are a higher vibration than your body may be accustomed to; therefore, be sure to ground yourself before and after working in your records. There are many ways to get grounded, such as: going outdoors, eating a healthy protein snack with intention, drinking a cool glass of water, or focusing on your body to feel the energy. You can become more consciously grounded by doing the Tripod Grounding Meditation again.

Practice makes it easier to go deeper into your records and start to receive information. Remember:

- Take a few breaths to center in your heart, ground yourself, and then connect.
- Read the Intention for Clarity Prayer, Step 1
- Write out a few simple questions, Step 2.
- Open the records using the given Sacred Access Prayer, Step 3.
- Once you feel the Akashic Column of Light around you, you may ask your questions.
- Record the answers in your journal.
- Fill yourself with your highest energy, Step 4.
- Close your records using the Akashic Records Closing Prayer, Step 5.

HOW DID IT FEEL TO OPEN YOUR RECORDS?

You will become more attuned to its energy each time you enter the Akasha. You'll want to build your relationship with the record keepers, to allow yourself to feel their love for you, and so that you learn to trust that they will always assist you on your human journey. They only wish to help us fulfill the souls' plan, because our deepest desire is to do so.

The energy of the Akasha is quite light compared to the heavy energy we live in on our planet. The more you enter your records, the brighter and lighter the energy becomes, so you will want to clear out your energy field and create firm boundaries from the inside out, using the tools you've learned in the previous chapters. You're learning to access a higher-vibration field and hold it in your body. Our bodies do not normally vibrate at such a high frequency, and growing used to that new high vibration takes time.

When doing healing work in the Akasha, you are clearing lower vibrations, which can contribute to tiredness. It's like exercising; you must keep building your energetic muscles. Think of a light bulb: outside your records, you are a thirty-watt bulb; inside your records, you are a 200-watt bulb. And when you close your records, it takes time to acclimate to the world around you. The energy feels light, warm, and embracing when you are in the Akasha. When you close your record, you drop back into our dimension, which is much heavier.

AM I REALLY IN MY AKASHIC RECORDS?

The one question I always hear in my live workshops is: "Am I really in my Akashic Records?" When we first start accessing our Akashic Records, we are still determining if it's really our record keepers that we hear and feel. It is a process of discernment.

Sometimes, we might think we aren't clairvoyant because we don't see many pictures. We may think the voice we hear sounds like our own, which leads us to believe that it can't be the record keepers; maybe it's our egos getting involved by giving us a lot of advice. So here are some tips you can use to work through the doubts and move into trust.

When you doubt if you are in your records, the simplest things to do are:

- Close your records, then recenter yourself and ground your body to be fully present.

- Go through the Akashic Knowing Five-Step Wisdom Prayer System again. Remember to always read and focus on the words of the prayer as you open your records. Refrain from memorizing the opening prayer. The Intention for Clarity Prayer is particularly beneficial when you are in doubt.
- Focus your questions on one subject to receive a bigger picture, so you can feel the depth of the answers. This process will help to relieve doubt. When you think, *I wouldn't have thought of that*, then you can be assured the answer isn't coming from you but instead is Divinely guided.
- Start with simple questions that aren't life changing. As with all new tools, you need to practice using them to become proficient in wielding them. An example of a simple question, when you are starting out, is: "Is there physical exercise or food that would be beneficial for me today" Not, "What is my life purpose?" or "Should I get a divorce and sell the house?"
- Try asking your questions differently or ask the beings of light for assistance in formulating new questions.
- Pay close attention to how the answers feel in your body. Do they give you goosebumps or tears in your eyes?
- Move out of your head by writing the question down in your journal and then letting the answers flow.

Learning to read your records is a process and practice. The best way to deepen into this work is to open your records every day and ask questions. Do some of the guided visualizations from the previous chapter once you've opened your records, to help you move deeper into the Akasha. As you spend fifteen to twenty minutes in the records doing the visualizations, the energy strengthens and it's easier to get answers to your questions.

Part Three

I'm so happy you are learning to access your personal Akashic wisdom. I hope to hear all about the experiences you have and the information you learn from your Akashic Record Keepers. In the next chapter, we will share about some of the galactic wisdom that we can receive when working in our Akashic Records.

OUR GALACTIC ORIGINS

*D*o you look up at the stars at night and think, *Maybe I'm from one of those stars or planets?* Do you ever dream about living in another world? Many of us have watched fantasy movies and felt so connected to the world we see on the screen that we are sure we've had lives there in another life.

I have always felt connected to water. Now I know I was a whale, a dolphin, and even a mermaid in other lives. As I described earlier in this book, the record keepers told me I was a whale in the distant past.

The fascinating part about working in the Akasha is that we can ask questions about otherworldly lives. I love teaching people to access the Akasha because there is so much information there for you.

Of course, we love to ask the big questions about our purpose and whether we have a soul contract with another person. But we also can ask whether we have lived on another planet or in another dimension. We can ask, "Was I an angel in another lifetime?"

If you have a deep connection to the water, you may wish to ask your record keepers, "Have I ever been on a water world as a mermaid or merman?" You could also ask for the name of that watery planet.

Part Three

Many of my students remember various lifetimes where they've lived in other physical forms that were not at all similar to our human condition. Our record keepers say that we enjoy living in different places and dimensions, in other types of worlds, and in many forms.

When I have the time, I go into my record to explore some of my other lifetimes. I'm curious to discover what I was and where I've traveled. On one of my explorations, the record keepers showed me a planet resembling a big, dry rock. When I zoomed in closer, I could tell it was an uninhabitable, dry planet. Then I zoomed in even further and saw a small hole and a giant insect. I could see myself crawling further and further down into the hole in this rock planet. As I got deeper into the hole, space suddenly opened. I found myself in a vast, hollow place with a whole world at its center.

In that life, I was in the body of a species of walking-stick insect. The other beings looked like different species of praying mantis, like the ones we have here on Earth, but they were much larger, about the size of a large dog or even a pony.

As I experienced that life, I realized I was communicating telepathically with the other life forms. We were creating and building together. It was a whole ecosystem and society with families and communities. The record keepers shared with me that even though the world looked very simple, it was a sophisticated society with advanced technology that served them well in this dry world. They also had the ability to transport themselves to other worlds.

The record keepers told me that many of the ETs or aliens that visit Earth would look more like giant insects than humans. They've shared that only a few otherworldly beings in the multiverse look like humans. Some have human forms and different sorts of faces or heads, but many have a variety of arms and legs different from our own.

GALACTIC RECORDS

Have you ever wondered if you're a star seed? When I asked in the Akashic Records about us being star seeds, which means we are from different stars or planets, I was told that we are *all* star seeds. In other words, no one comes directly to Earth. Instead, we start our journey as vast souls out in the multiverse, enjoying the spaciousness and often creating places or planets for ourselves, our friends, and our soul family members to inhabit. So, if you can imagine that you are a vast soul that can create worlds, then you're imagining an aspect of your soul self that we rarely think of.

Again, imagine you've spent many of your past lifetimes in the tenth or twelfth dimension. You've been in angelic form or alien forms in other dimensions, knowing that we are indeed one with the higher-vibrational dimensions. We know there is no separation and that we are all part of Source energy and, therefore, all one with each other. We realize that what we do to ourselves affects the rest of the community and world. Those are vastly different types of lives because we do not believe we are separate. The work we do is often for the greater good and the collective.

When you know that you are so much more than a simple human living only one life, then you can start to imagine that you are a star seed. You might have lived on the dog star Sirius or the Pleiades. Maybe you came through the stargate in Orion's belt from another galaxy. You may have lived on Arcturus and arrived here at this time in history to help humanity move from the old patterns of war to the higher vibration of peace and eventually on into awakening.

The Akashic Record Keepers tell me that the Galactic Akasha is opening. We have been waiting a long time for this new energy alignment with the galactic center. Many of us who have been here as lightworkers have been waiting since the year 2000, or earlier, but it's finally happening.

Part Three

That means we will have the ability to access higher vibrational information and memories more easily. When I first started accessing the Akashic Records, we thought that there were only Akashic Records for humans. And as I've gone deeper into the Akasha over these last thirty years, I've realized that there is often information about our star seed lineage in our records.

More recently, I've channeled many galactic prayers for humanity. Each access prayer relates to a different planet or world. And so, it helps us to understand our souls' journey more fully as we discover the star seed lineage access prayers that most resonate with us.

Prayers are from worlds such as Sirius, Arcturus, the Pleiades, Orion, and the angelic realm; there is even one for the galactic traveler. Recently, the record keepers have given me two more access prayers. One is from Lyra, and the newest is from Andromeda, which is not only another world but a whole different galaxy. These galactic Akashic Records have recently started to open so that we can access more information about who we are: ancient and infinite beings with galactic pasts.

CREATING THIS EARTH EXPERIENCE

Have you wondered why your life is so hard? Why do you struggle to make a discussion? Why are we so worried about money? You may have thought, *Why would I write a whole soul plan and then forget about it?* Or you think, *I would never pick that family! Those people were horrible.* The answer to these conscious and unconscious questions is that it's part of the game we came to play.

We are at a point in history where we can access and understand who we are as great galactic beings who created this third-dimensional Earth. The new information you receive will assist you in knowing who you are in the bigger picture of your soul's journey. It will help you comprehend the idea that we chose to have these challenging experiences of feeling separation, pain, and trauma. We genuinely wanted to lose ourselves in the matrix of this world that many of us created.

As infinite galactic beings who have taken many forms in many dimensions, we have roamed the multiverse forever. We wanted a brand-new experience that was never available to us. And so, we created this third-dimensional Earth. We wanted to completely believe that this is all there is. It is up to us alone to find our way home. This is why we created a world where we believe we are separate and alone. We believe there is no real outside help from angels or Divine assistance.

Imagine that you wanted to make a game of deep immersion coming down from the 12th or 8th dimension. That was an intense dive into humanness that you took. That is indeed what we have done and what we are living.

THE MAZE OF LIFE

When you were a child, did you ever go into a giant maze at the pumpkin farm on Halloween? You might have thought it would be fun and easy, but then you get lost and scared. This maze was taller than you, and you couldn't see anyone else. Then, as it got dark, it was even scarier. You knew you had to find your way out, or you might be stuck there for a long time. When you're a small child, you believe you must find the way, forgetting that your parents or older siblings are looking for you to help you out.

That's similar to what we're experiencing in our life. We wanted to find our way home, but we forgot that there is help in physical and in energetic forms, such as the Akashic Record Keepers and our angel guides.

Our bigger picture here on Earth is only a tiny portion of who we are. We are galactic beings, finding our way home by learning the truth of who we are as Divine and infinite souls playing a game.

Part Three

LIGHTWORKERS ARE HERE TO HELP

There are thousands of lightworkers on Earth now to remember the truth of who we are. We are here to help all of humanity remember by assisting them in unlocking the blocks we have placed on our galactic memories. We are here to make it possible for our friends and family to move to a higher level of consciousness.

It's time to stop waiting for someone to save us. We must step into our power as infinite galactic beings so we can get down to helping those in the world who need our talents, stories, and wisdom.

Through access to your Akasha, you can move into the quantum field, outside of time and space, to clear energy blocks and reclaim your gifts and the truth of who you are. Many of you hold within your bodies and energy fields the keys and codes that are now ready to be activated, to help everyone elevate the lower levels of consciousness experienced by most people on Earth.

The Akashic Record Keepers want to thank you for remembering who you are as a powerful, galactic soul. They are grateful for all your work to awaken humanity.

In the final chapter, we will share thoughts about our collective next steps.

AWAKENING TO THE NEW EARTH

As we raise our vibration and become more conscious, we start to feel the connectedness of the soul to everything around us. Many can feel this connectedness to their higher self and to the Akashic Record Keepers.

What can we do right now? The first step is to transform our experiences and challenges by raising our vibration as we become more conscious. Next, it's time to clear away the low-vibrational energy so we can understand the bigger picture of the plan our souls wrote.

Finally, and most importantly, remember you are never alone.

You have countless souls as a support system, including guardian angels, loved ones who have crossed over, archangels who support all of humanity, and your own personal Akashic Record Keepers.

You are on a journey of awakening, and it's time to become more fully conscious and for your physical body to be more powerful. When you realize you are one of many players in a large-scale movie, you start to let go of so many old beliefs that have stopped you from becoming the person you incarnated to be.

You can then untangle yourself from emotional pain, fear, doubt, and judgment. As you do this, you will start unraveling and eliminating some old energetic programs that kept you stuck on the hamster's wheel for thousands of years. Your old stories—your programs of separation, victimhood, and unworthiness—hold most of humanity in low-vibrational levels.

OUR EARTH IS AWAKENING

The Earth herself, Gaia, is a sentient being who has become stuck in this third dimension. The exciting news is she is starting to awaken and break free. As she awakens, we will all awaken with greater ease. Imagine that our dear Mother Earth has been trapped in this third-dimensional vibration, and now we are cutting the ropes that tie her down. We are clearing and releasing old stories, programming, and patterns that have kept the Earth and humanity locked down.

Imagine Gaia as if she were a tethered balloon. As we cut the ropes and clear the programs, she will raise her vibration, and we'll float from the third dimension and into the fourth and then onward. Then, one year in the not-too-distant future, we'll even rise into the fifth dimension and possibly higher.

What will moving into the fourth and fifth dimensions be like? The Akashic Record Keepers say we will stop living in a world of anger, judgment, shame, guilt, fear, and survival. Instead, we will naturally be open to receiving love and feeling joy. The low vibrational emotions are part of what we, as infinite galactic beings, wrote into the energy programs that hold Gaia down in the third dimension.

As you raise your energy vibration and frequency, you shift how you see the world. As soon as we can start to move away from feeling like victims, we start acting differently. We move from worry, disappointment, and overwhelm into the higher vibrations of willingness and acceptance.

We are breaking through a barrier that has held humanity down for tens of thousands of years. Moving into hopefulness, enthusiasm, and happiness is an easy way to raise your vibration permanently.

As a people, we will awaken to a place of compassion and forgiveness for everyone around us. When we can forgive and love, we align with the vibration of freedom. When we notice peace and joy permeating the world, that is when we are in the fourth dimension.

When we start to create from the energy of happiness, enthusiasm, and love, we create the new Earth. We will find that we can manifest our heart's desires with greater ease. Instant manifestation will come online in the fourth dimension, and creating what your soul planned so long ago will become much easier.

YOU ARE THE ONE THAT YOU'VE BEEN WAITING FOR

We are doing it now, and you are helping by reading this book, learning to access your own Akashic Records, and doing your meditation and personal healing work. The Akashic Record Keepers tell us that this is how we will awaken as humanity and transform the world, changing from pain to hope to enlightenment.

Now that you understand your soul created a plan and stored it in the Akasha, you can shift that plan and make newer, bigger choices. This book has offered you the tools to free yourself from old beliefs and blocked energetic patterns. You can now create the life your heart and soul desire. Please know that you are a perfect, complete, and Divine soul.

Thank you so much for joining us in transforming the world. You are a blessing to all of us! The Akashic Record Keepers want you to know how

Part Three

grateful they are for the consciousness you are becoming and for the love, kindness, and joy that you share with others every day.

Much love and many blessings to you.

Lisa Barnett

MEET THE SACRED STORYTELLERS

LINDA BERGER is an Akashic Record teacher, consultant, author, strategic business coach, and founder of Akashic Record Business Coaching. Linda's secret sauce is being fluent in the language of business and the language of the soul. akashicrecordbusinesscoaching.com.

DR. KURT JOHNSON is the cofounder of Light on Light Press, an imprint dedicated to interspirituality. He is one of three co-editors of *Our Moment of Choice*, co-author of *The Coming Interspiritual Age*, *Nabokov's Blues*, and *Fine Lines*. Kurt cofounded The Interspiritual Dialogue with Br. Wayne Teasdale and is a member of the Evolutionary Leaders. lightonlight.us.

CAROLINE LAMBERT has been a mystic, intuitive, and sensitive since childhood. A freak accident filled with trauma and pain led her on a life changing journey.

STEPHANY LEONARD LEVINE is the founder of Empowering Evolution, Inc. She assists others in utilizing the tools of the Akashic Records and the Compass Life Management System. akashic.stevielevine.com.

REBEKA LOPEZ is an Akashic Record consultant, and a natural healer utilizing tarot, reiki, flower therapy and EFT. Her passion is to guide people so they may live a joyful life. livejoyously.net.

MARCIA LOWRY offers channeled energy healing and workshops through the Awakening Heart Center in Saint Paul. Sessions include Qigong sound, crystals, or EFT, to bring physical, spiritual, emotional, and ancestral healing. awakeningheartcenter.com.

SIOBHAN MAGUIRE is a sensitive empath who was diagnosed with cancer at age thirty-one and chose a completely holistic path to wellness, dedicating over 20 years to her work as a healer, coach, and therapist. healthyselftherapy.com.

JENNY MANNION healed seven years of diseases in three weeks and awakened to her purpose. She is an author, speaker, teacher, and healer inspiring self-love and manifesting the life we desire. jennymannion.com.

ERIKA OSMANN MASON is a certified consultant through the Akashic Knowing School of Wisdom. She helps people locate and transform low energy patterns in their chakra energy system, teaches people to feel their relationship energy dynamics so they can make informed relationship choices. She also helps people find peace with those who have crossed-over. lightfilledlife.com.

MICHELLE MCCLENNEN has spent the majority of her life in therapy healing from her ancestral lineage of traumatic abuse. Married thirty years and was a stay-at-home mother, Michelle is also a graduate of our nation's eldest mystery school, Delphi University. michellemcclennen.com.

SOPHIA MOON began writing at the age of eight and has been an avid journal writer. She is a reflexologist, hypnotherapist, singer/songwriter and painter. She studies meditation at templeoftheinnerself.org.

PAMELA NANCE has a master's degree in anthropology, researched the survival of consciousness after death, and has certifications in healing touch, past life regression, hypnotherapy, shamanism, and spiritual dowsing. pamelanance.com.

SANDY RAKOWITZ discovered an unspoken, intuitive language of trust, safety, and rapport with horses that inspired her life's work guiding others into their multidimensional gifts as coach, artist, and author. oneheartuniversity.com.

JENNIFER PEREZ SOLAR is a Samassati Colorlight practitioner, newborn care specialist, and teacher. Her psychic and mediumship gifts merge with her business expertise to show others how to be change agents and movement creators. allowandflow.com.

SHERYL A. STRADLING is an award-winning abstract artist and author of *Faith, Power, Joy*, a multi-generational memoir, and a contributor to *Journey of an Empath*, a collection of transformational stories. sherylstradling.com.

RENEE TERESA is a government employee who has pursued Akashic readings in her retirement. She uses the Akasha to transmute painful memories to allow positive, forward movement. intuitivehealingwithrenee.com.

DEVARA THUNDERBEAT is a multi award-winning musician, composer, author, teacher, speaker, 22 DNA activator, Reiki master, and a pioneer in sound healing. thunderbeat.com.

MEET THE AUTHOR

Lisa Barnett has devoted her life as an ordained minister and Divine channel to helping people connect to their divinity and receive the soul guidance they are searching for to heal and transform their lives. As a Religious Science Certified Practitioner, R.S.C.P., she offered healing prayer treatment to the congregations and served as vice president on the board of directors of Golden Gate Center for Spiritual Living.

With her master's degree in Transpersonal Education, she founded Akashic Knowing School of Wisdom, an internationally recognized school where students can learn to access their soul wisdom in their Akashic Records along with numerous healing tools, meditation, and prayer systems. Lisa has taught thousands of students worldwide and has helped to train and certify dozens of Akashic consultants and teachers.

Lisa has more than thirty years of experience in the spiritual healing forum and is a master of many healing modalities. Her specialty is empowering individuals to find greater fulfillment, happiness, abundance, and health. She assists by helping them align with their soul path, understand their soul's plan, including soul contracts, karmic patterns and vows, enabling them to transform with greater ease.

Lisa is the bestselling author of *Your Soul Has a Plan: Awaken to Your Life Purpose through the Akashic Records*, *The Infinite Wisdom of the Akashic Records* and *From Questioning to Knowing: 73 Prayers to Transform Your Life*. She has developed many programs to help people experience lasting transformation, including ten written and auditory courses, dozens of meditations, and frequent webinars to teach people around the world how to access their Akashic Record. The goal of the programs and books is to share the tools and prayers from the Akashic Records to help her clients and students at a soul level create the life their heart and soul desires.

Learn more at https://akashicknowing.com.

Made in the USA
Columbia, SC
13 August 2023